On This Island

KEITH H. LANG

SCOTT B. COMINGS

All proceeds from the sale of this book go to The Nature Conservancy.

Once again, this book is dedicated to
the late Captain John R. Lewis
and to all those who have worked to preserve Block Island
and to the future generations who will inherit it.

Table of Contents

Introduction   vi

A Brief History of Conservation on Block Island   vii

Acknowledgements   xi

Foreword   xv

Important Things to Keep in Mind While Enjoying These Trails   xvi

Area 1: Clay Head Trail   1

Area 2: Hodge Family Wildlife Preserve   7

Area 3: Meadow Hill Greenway   11

The Greenway Trail System   15

Area 4: Great Salt Pond to Beacon Hill Road Link   17

Area 5: South Beacon Hill Road & Nathan Mott Park Trails   21

Area 6: Turnip Farm & Elaine Loffredo Preserve Trails   25

Area 7: Old Mill Road & Cooneymus Road Link to
Rodman's Hollow & Black Rock Trails   29

Area 8: Fresh Pond Trail   35

Area 9: Fresh Swamp & Payne Farm Trail   39

Area 10: Win Dodge & Dickens Farm Trails   43

Color Photos   48

Short Hikes   65

Other Conservation Areas of Interest   69

Conservation Groups Working on Block Island   72

Animal and Plant Species Lists   75

Index   90

Authors / Production Team   95

Look, stranger, on this island now
The leaping light for your delight discovers,
Stand stable here
And silent be,
That through the channels of the ear
May wander like a river
The swaying sound of the sea.

—*W. H. Auden*

Introduction

BY CHRISTOPHER LITTLEFIELD & ADRIAN MITCHELL

This guide is a tribute to the people who have contributed their time and effort to protect the land and create the walking trails of Block Island. When we were growing up, we believed that the entire island was open to us and that the natural world was everywhere we turned. At Clay Head or on the Greenway trails, it is still possible to feel that way and to imagine what this place was like when our ancestors first saw it more than three hundred years ago.

It is important to preserve the Island's heritage, not just buildings and objects, but the land that has sustained us for so many generations. Not many communities in North America have been able to do this, but Block Island has, which is one of the many reasons that we are proud to be citizens here. The preservation did not just happen; it came about because people cared and had a positive, can-do attitude. As you walk these trails, please remember what it took to make this opportunity possible. Those who are dedicated and determined in their efforts to preserve Block Island have demonstrated what can be accomplished when people rise to a challenge and work together toward a common goal.

CHRISTOPHER LITTLEFIELD is the Director of Landscape Programs for The Nature Conservancy's Rhode Island office. He is descended from an early Island family and grew up here during summers. Christopher has lived on the Island year-round since 1982 and was the first person hired by The Nature Conservancy to do full-time conservation work on Block Island in 1991.

ADRIAN MITCHELL works as a preserve caretaker for The Nature Conservancy. He is a graduate of the Block Island School and for many years was the town highway supervisor. Adrian lives on a farm that has been in his family for more than 200 years and is now protected in its current state as a result of his generous effort.

vi

A Brief History of Conservation on Block Island

For as long as people have inhabited Block Island, they have needed a conservation ethic to survive. Wind and weather, time and tide, and the marshalling of limited resources are continual reminders of a finite place, isolated and apart, surrounded by an ever-changing sea. It is a fragile landscape where missteps can be devastating; therefore, it must be treated with care.

The first inhabitants were the Manisseans, a Native American people, who established one of the earliest known year-round settlements in southern New England more than 2500 years ago. Their village was located along the shore of Great Salt Pond, and they lived almost exclusively from what they took from the sea. The archeological remains from their long habitation suggest they lived well and simply, leaving the landscape largely undisturbed. According to an archeologist who studied their village, "It was a Garden of Eden, rich with resources."

When European explorers first observed Block Island in the Sixteenth Century, they noted that it was heavily forested. In the decades following the first settlement in 1661, the early settlers cut down the trees for fuel, housing, and other basic needs. Only by discovering peat for fuel—until coal became readily available in the early 1800s—could people continue to live on the Island.

For generations thereafter, the Island people were inspired, by inclination or circumstance, to live in relative harmony with nature, sustaining themselves by harvesting the land and the sea. Beginning in the later part of the Nineteenth Century, tourism supplemented their economy. While many factors combined to bring about the mid-Twentieth-Century decline of fishing and farming as a way of life, the essence of life connected to the natural world remained.

The modern conservation era can be traced to two women, who each in her own way left a lasting legacy. Miss Elizabeth Dickens lived her entire 84 years on the remote southwest corner of the Island. She kept a bird diary, meticulously recording her sightings every day from 1912 until her death in 1963. For many years, she also taught bird lore to the Island schoolchildren, imbuing in them an appreciation for wildlife and its relationship to the land. She inspired many, caused them to look at their surroundings in a more gentle way, and planted the seeds of the present conservation effort.

The first property to be permanently protected was the result of a gift to the community in 1941 by Lucretia Mott Ball. The Greenway runs through this area, which she named the Nathan Mott Park after her father. Though the Island's agricultural past was fast fading at that time, the land outside the two harbors was still open and undeveloped, and the full impact of her foresight and generosity would become evident only decades later.

As the nation put World War II behind and began to attain unprecedented prosperity, Block Island remained quiet and "undiscovered" until the early 1970s. Change was inevitable, however, as the Island's convenient location made it easily accessible by ferries, planes, and pleasure boats. Block Island is only a half-day trip for more than 20 million people, yet one can still feel tremendous isolation here.

The resultant development pressures made it apparent that action must be taken to protect the health of the ecosystem and maintain the Island's rural character. To realize these goals, the community, led by Captain John R. Lewis, formed the Block Island Conservancy in 1972 and began the preservation of Rodman's Hollow Preserve. As the work increased and the projects became more complicated, the Block Island Conservancy soon after enlisted the assistance of The Nature Conservancy. This international organization has become a permanent partner in conservation on the Island and maintains a local office, which was opened in 1991.

The town has been a big part of the conservation effort, with townspeople taxing themselves through bond issues to preserve land. When these funds proved inadequate, Keith Lewis began the movement in 1986 to set up the Block Island Land Trust, a municipal organization, now funded by a three percent transfer fee on real estate transactions.

Other groups that have played major roles are the Audubon Society of Rhode Island, the United States Fish & Wildlife Service, and the Rhode Island Department of Environmental Management. Together, this partnership has been successful in preserving more than 40 percent of the Island, protecting a number of the key ecological sites and scenic vistas, and increasing and enhancing public access.

Is that enough? Are these efforts sufficient to protect the Island's fragile ecosystem and single water source? Since the local economy is reliant on tourism, has enough land been conserved to insure the preservation of the rural landscape that is so attractive to visitors? Is there ample critical habitat left to sustain the endangered species that continue to survive on Block Island but are disappearing from many other places in the region?

Many ancient cultures believed that to hurt the earth was to hurt one's self. As the early European settlers discovered, actions taken simply to address immediate needs can have unseen and potentially perilous consequences. The lesson of Block Island is: if a place is understood and respected by its people, it has a chance of being preserved. There are people involved in conservation on Block Island who believe the Island is a microcosm of the planet. For these individuals, success or failure in absorbing and living this lesson not only impacts this Island but also places far beyond these shores.

The Lapham Family created the first walking trails near Clay Head; they opened their property and maintained it themselves for the benefit of the public. It was their inspiration that led to the formation of trail systems throughout the Island, which were designed to make land conservation tangible and allow everyone, those who live here or visit, to have access to some of the most remote and beautiful places. Few shore areas elsewhere offer such access. It is possible here because of the generosity and hard work of many people who care deeply about Block Island. By respecting these trails and the lands they run through, you can contribute to the preservation of an island—and an ethic.

Though it is heartening to note that the land-preservation effort continues to flourish, enjoying widespread support in the community and the appreciation of visitors, the importance of also preserving a conservation ethic has only grown, not diminished. The ecological health of Block Island cannot be measured only in acres preserved, but also in the stewardship of the land and what happens to the landscape as a whole.

In the five years since this book was first published, development pressure has increased, real estate prices have skyrocketed, and those concerned about the Island's future well-being have turned their attention toward the built environment. There are more and more examples of individuals pushing the envelope to capitalize personally on the benefits brought about by conservation by building large houses out of proportion to their surroundings or pushing money-making initiatives that threaten the balance between economic opportunity and the pristine natural beauty upon which it is based.

This situation has been compounded by the continuing inability of the outside world to comprehend or appreciate the Island's desire to promote a conservation ethic. Time after time, state and federal government bodies thwart the near unanimous wishes of the community to protect its resources, and side instead with an individual's perceived right to realize private gain at our expense. While the concept of individual rights has been central to defining what it means to be an American, it is inconceivable that the Founding Fathers intended these rights to subsume and supersede those of the community.

If Block Island is to continue to be a refuge for wildlife and humans alike, a place where the environment and the local economy can flourish in harmony, then the time has come to assert and preserve an ethic—a value bred of hard experience and sacrifice—by educating those both near and far of its importance to the future of the Island.

The dedication stone in Loffredo Preserve

Acknowledgements

Similar to most of the projects we have been involved in on Block Island, this edition, like the one that preceded it, was a team effort.

Upon first seeing *On This Island*, Eva Anderson of Symbio Design expressed an interest in working on such a project. When we found ourselves in the happy position of needing a second edition, we remembered her remark and offered her the opportunity. Fortunately for us, she took us up on it, and this version of the guide is a testament to her wonderful talent for layout and design. We also greatly appreciate her keeping us on track, guiding the completed copy through the publishing process, and seeing the project through to completion.

We are further fortunate to have Robert Ellis Smith, or simply Bob to us, agree to serve as our editor. Bob is a Block Island resident who has many talents and interests: he is an author; the publisher of the newsletter *Privacy Journal*; past President of the Block Island Conservancy; and member of the Town Council. He is the person most responsible for smoothly incorporating the changes and new information related to the second edition.

In addition to being a valued staff member of the Block Island Office of The Nature Conservancy, Charlotte Herring helped in many ways with this project, particularly proof-reading and facilitating communication among all of the parties involved in putting it together.

If there had not been a successful first edition, there would be no need for a second. We would be remiss not to acknowledge again the wonderful contributions of those who helped us launch the effort the first time around. They are: Dennis Wolkoff, Johno Sisto, Christopher Littlefield, Martha Ball, Bob Downie, Marcy Hall, Todd Macalister, Adrian Mitchell, Beatrix Mattyasovszky and Norman Specht.

Special thanks goes to all the people who donated land easements and property to allow the dream of Greenway trails to become a reality. They are: Jens Risom and family; the Lapham Family; the late Captain John R. and Alyce Lewis and family; the Beacon Hill Homeowners Association; Kurt and Erica Tonner; the Erlanger Family; the Harrison Family,

Christopher Walling; the Town of New Shoreham; Hal Oppenheimer; the Jules and Doris Stein Foundation; the Reed and Barrell families, Burt and Melanie King, Robert Loffredo, Peter and the late Shirley Wood; Dan and Jean Larkin; the Guerry Family, the Asch Family; Michael Wagner, Suzanne Wagner, the Peckham Farm Homeowners Association; Harriet and the late William Phelan; Blake and Michele Phelan; the Panero Family; the Ocean View Foundation; Al and the late Norma Starr; the Murphy Family; the Cormier Family; the Attwood Family; the Jones Family; Harry Spryut; Judith and Charles Cyronak; F. Norris and Nancy Pike; the late William Lewis; and the late Margaret Meiss.

We would like to also thank those people who were most responsible for helping to create a system of walking trails on Block Island in the first place: Elise and the late F. David Lapham; Peter and the late Shirley Wood; Donald and Dorothy McCluskey; Robert Smith; Deborah Penn; Christopher Littlefield; Laura Rosenzweig; David Lewis; and Keith Lewis. Special thanks go to Gene Hall, who cut most of the Greenway trails and did an amazing job of making the lines on a map become interesting and enjoyable walking trails.

And finally, thanks go out to all those who purchased the first edition, for their assistance and support. Since this was almost entirely a volunteer effort, nearly 100 percent of the proceeds ($16,900 netted from the original version) went to The Nature Conservancy for the purpose of maintaining and enhancing the trail system.

A Greenway trail marker

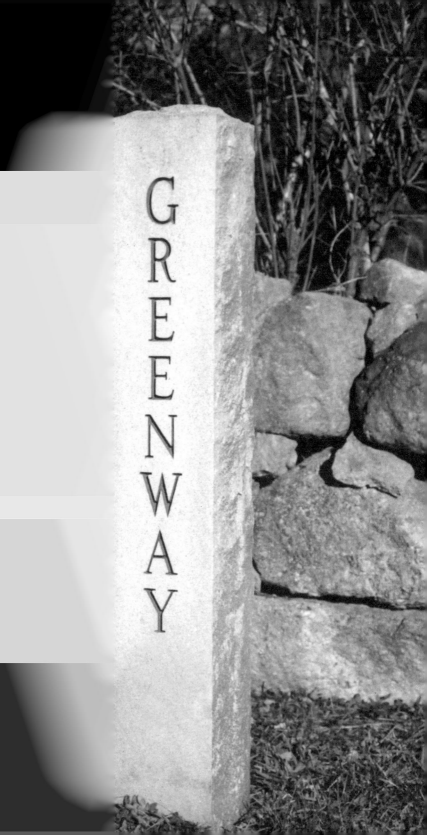

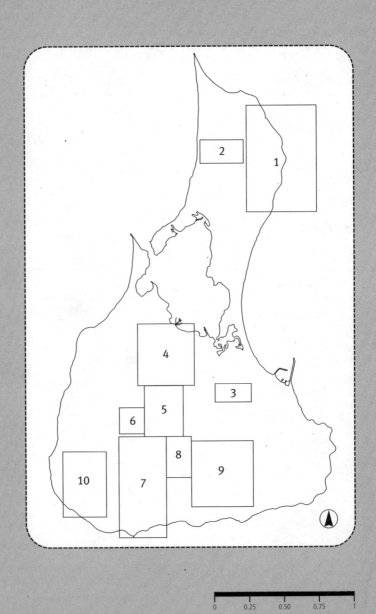

Foreword

The trail guide that follows is just that: a guide. Too often in our harried society, people concentrate only on the getting there and not on the process or path taken. We have tried to provide enough information to be of interest and assistance, leaving you to discover for yourself the beauty of this Island and the trails that help to make it accessible.

The paths are described in distinct sections, but we have endeavored to make clear, when appropriate, how and where they interconnect with other trails. It is important to keep in mind that these trails can be more than a walk through the natural world of Block Island; they also provide a way of getting from place to place.

One of our greatest challenges was to approximate walking times and the degree of difficulty presented by each individual pathway. People walk at different paces; what one person perceives as challenging may be a casual stroll to someone else. The walking times listed reflect the amount of time we think it would take to cover a section of trail if the walker is stopping frequently to observe the things encountered along the way. Almost all of the levels of difficulty of the paths are defined as "moderate" because much of the Island is hilly and almost all of the trails contain steep slopes and uneven ground. The only trail that we qualify as "easy" is the path on the Hodge Family Wildlife Preserve, which is almost level throughout and presents less difficult terrain.

These trails were created for everyone to enjoy, and we hope you avail yourself of the opportunity to do so.

Important Things to Keep in Mind
While Enjoying These Trails

BICYCLES AND HORSES ARE PROHIBITED ON TRAILS

Biking and horseback riding are a wonderful way to enjoy Block Island
—but not on these trails. Both activities contribute to erosion and present
safety concerns. These uses are prohibited on all walking trails and
constitute trespassing. Biking and horseback riding are allowed on all
publicly accessible dirt roads.

LYME DISEASE IS COMMON TO BLOCK ISLAND

It is strongly suggested that you take proper precautions before setting
out so that you avoid deer ticks, which are carriers of Lyme disease. The
disease can cause persistent fevers or debilitating symptoms. It is advis-
able to wear long pants tucked into socks, stay clear of tall grass and
overhanging vegetation, and check for ticks after any outdoor activities.
Light-colored clothing is also recommended, as it makes it easier to spot
ticks, which are smaller than a pinpoint. Further information about the
disease is available at the Block Island Medical Center or The Nature
Conservancy office.

OBSERVE RIGHTS OF PROPERTY OWNERS

While much of the trail system proceeds through public land, a signifi-
cant portion is open to the public through the generosity of private
landowners. Please respect their privacy by staying on the trails, keeping
noise to a minimum, and observing the rules for appropriate use.

KEEP PETS LEASHED

If not properly monitored, pets can kill or harm wildlife and disturb the
ability of others to enjoy the trails. They also can get lost or transport
disease-bearing ticks indoors. Please clean up after your pets.

BEACHES, DUNES, AND BLUFFS ARE FRAGILE

Beaches, dunes, and bluffs are part of the Island's natural defense against
storms and the sea. Please stay clear of dunes and bluffs, and avoid tram-
pling sensitive vegetation, which holds these features in place. Many
plants and animals that depend on the beach cannot survive without
your help.

KEEP TRAILS CLEAN

If you bring paper, cans, bottles, or other items with you, please be sure to dispose of any trash or waste properly. If you see litter on the trails, you can help out by picking it up and taking it with you.

BE AWARE OF POISON IVY

Poison ivy flourishes on Block Island and is located in many places along the trails. For those unfamiliar with it, poison ivy is a vine with three leaves that are often shiny. The best approach is to follow the maxim

"leaves of three, let it be." If you do come in contact, scrub the infected area as soon as possible with a strong soap and water. As with ticks, if you stay in the middle of the trail and avoid direct contact with any vegetation, you will minimize your risk.

HUNTING POLICY

Shotgun hunting is a concern only on weekdays between November and February. Hunting is allowed at Clay Head and on the Jones Property (south of Rodman's Hollow) with landowner permission, and these areas should be avoided during the week. On all other trails, hunting is not allowed. To play it safe, it is best not to walk on the trails on hunting days. If you decide to walk anyway at these times, please wear orange. Keep in mind that the beaches and roadsides are wonderful alternative places to walk, especially at this time of year. If you have any questions regarding hunting on Block Island, we advise you to call the police department, Town Hall, or The Nature Conservancy office.

DON'T FORGET WATER, SUNSCREEN AND INSECT REPELLENT

Whenever going on a hike it is always good practice to bring the items listed above, for they will ensure an excellent experience.

REMEMBER

If you respect this trail system by observing these simple rules, you guarantee your own enjoyment of the experience and make it possible for those following you to enjoy it as well.

WALKING TIME	1.5 hours entrance 1 to 3 or .5 hour entrance 2 to Clay Head bluff
DISTANCE	2 miles entrance 1 to 3 or .7 mile entrance 2 to Clay Head bluff
FROM OLD HARBOR FERRY LANDING	3 miles

DEGREE OF DIFFICULTY

Moderate-some steep slopes & uneven ground

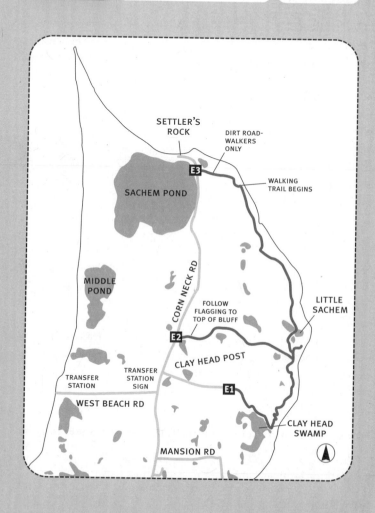

SETTLER'S ROCK

DIRT ROAD-WALKERS ONLY

E3

WALKING TRAIL BEGINS

SACHEM POND

MIDDLE POND

CORN NECK RD

FOLLOW FLAGGING TO TOP OF BLUFF

LITTLE SACHEM

E2

CLAY HEAD POST

TRANSFER STATION

TRANSFER STATION SIGN

E1

WEST BEACH RD

CLAY HEAD SWAMP

MANSION RD

Roadways

Trail

Coastal Features

E Trail Entrance

0   0.25   0.50

CLAY HEAD TRAIL

LOCATION There are three places to access the Clay Head Trail off Corn Neck Road. The first can be found just north and east of the transfer station sign where there is a gray post marked "Clay Head Trail." We encourage people to leave cars here and walk, as the dirt road is actually private. Parking and bike racks are available, however, about four-tenths of a mile down the dirt lane, near the fence marking the trailhead.

The second access point, which was added in 2005, is directly off Corn Neck Road, on the right, two-tenths of a mile north of the Clay Head Trail post. Persons who want to use this entrance should park either on the side of the road, or preferably, at the Hodge Family Wildlife Preserve lot located 150 feet further north on the left.

To locate the third access point, follow Corn Neck Road north until you come to the last dirt road on your right opposite Sachem Pond, before the main road bends to the left toward Settlers Rock. Follow the dirt lane for about one-quarter of a mile, until you see the walking trail opening on your left.

HISTORY OF TRAIL The walking trail system on Block Island was born here on Corn Neck Road in the 1960s when F. David and Elise Lapham cut paths through their property, which they called "Bluestone," and welcomed the public to use them. The area became known as "The Maze," and the Laphams maintained it for the benefit of the public. If you think it is impossible to get lost on Block Island, think again. We have known many people who have become disoriented here, and one of Keith's relatives, who shall remain nameless, missed the boat while going for a "brief walk in The Maze" to pass the time before the ferry left.

This guide will describe only the Clay Head Trail, the path that runs primarily north to south, paralleling the bluff, and the trail that connects the Hodge Family Wildlife Preserve to the Clay Head Bluff. If you choose to branch out into the maze, you are welcome, but you are also on your own. To preserve the enchantment of the area, these trails are not shown on any map. If you become disoriented, remember that the Clay Head Trail is to the east. It may take a while, but heading in that direction and listening for the sounds of the ocean will bring you to the marked path, and you can continue your walk with the confidence of knowing your location. There are approximately 12 miles of trails in the maze system, running to the west of the main trail and frequently intersecting it.

This property was permanently protected in the late 1970s. It was one of the first major conservation projects on Block Island. Clay Head is one of the most beautiful places on the Island — or anywhere, for that matter. The Laphams cannot be commended enough for their generosity, hospitality, and foresight. Not only did they give a protective easement over this entire area, but their gift also qualified the State of Rhode Island for federal matching funds that were used in the preservation of sections of Rodman's Hollow, Clay Head, and the Mohegan Bluffs.

DESCRIPTION OF TRAIL The Clay Head Trail walk can be done in a number of ways. Beginning from the southern entrance, one can walk out to the beach and back, continue on to the end of the trail and make a round trip, or proceed north out to Corn Neck Road and complete a loop back by road to the dirt lane and trailhead.

Regardless of how ambitious you feel, there is a lot to see in Clay Head Preserve. Heading east from the trailhead toward the ocean, you will see some big trees, sycamore maples, which mark the site of an old farmhouse. Look in the holes of the trees for nesting birds, such as the black-capped chickadee, yellow-shafted flicker, and Carolina wren. The trail then proceeds through a meadow with open views across Clay Head Swamp to the Atlantic Ocean. You can see Old Harbor to the south. The path proceeds downhill and parallels the swamp. Across the water are the Littlefield and Ball Farms, two of the best remaining examples of the saltwater farms that once extended up and down the coast of the Island.

Clay Head Swamp has only native fish, such as brown bullhead and golden shiner, which is rare for any pond in New England. As you go downhill toward the swamp, you will notice many wetland plants as you cross a bridge. In the late spring, listen for the "Sweet, sweet, sweet, I'm so sweet" of the yellow warbler. Just before the beach, the trail heads to the left and north. You might want to take a break and explore the beach.

Carolina Wren

If you do, look up at the bluff and notice all the holes; these are home to the bank swallow. If you are here in the summer, watch for them darting in and out of these holes in the bank. Further down the beach, to the north, you will find the remains of "Pots and Kettles." These are glacially formed underground water channels composed of rocks and sand, which have been fused by iron oxides and exposed as the bluff erodes.

From the beach, the trail climbs and then levels off, paralleling the bluff all the way until the path ends at a dirt lane, which leads back out to Corn Neck Road and beyond to Settlers Rock and Sandy Point. Along the way are majestic views and a number of overlooks where you can see the waves crashing below. Be careful not to get too close to the bank, as the bluff is fragile and undercut, and it is a long drop to the beach. There is no better evidence of the severe erosion of these clay bluffs than the point where the trail parallels Little Sachem Pond.

The eastern section of this pond washed out in 2005. The Nature Conservancy had worked closely with the Laphams in the mid-1990's, and again in 2002, to save it by installing a drainage pipe to control over-flow and re-vegetate the area to slow erosion. Unfortunately, the water pressure became too great and overwhelmed those remediation meas-ures and washed over the bluff to the beach below, creating a gully as it went. Fortunately, the western portion of this exquisite hourglass-shaped pond remains intact and is an excellent place to see great blue herons or yellow-crowned night herons. The new trail goes through what was the middle of the pond but is now dry. Be sure to look east when crossing what was the pond and see nature's power.

When the Hodge Property was preserved in 2002, it became possible to connect conservation lands from east to west by walking trails. The second entrance off Corn Neck Road to the bluffs at Clay Head was created in 2005 on part of the Lapham Property known by the family as the "Long Lot." This is called the Long Lot Trail and you need to follow closely the orange blazes that distinguish it from the other trails in this part of The Maze. As you go, you might note some of the mature deciduous trees, a variety of exotic species that were planted in the 1960s and 1970s by David and Elise Lapham. You might also keep an eye out for Cooper's hawks, which nest in the area. This species was decimated by DDT, but has made an amazing comeback recently, starting nesting again on Block Island in 2004. As the trail continues to wind along, you will see some nice meadows containing common milkweed that are a great place to look for migratory monarch butterflies in the fall. When the Long Lot Trail connects to the Clay Head Trail at a point just to the south of Little Sachem, you can either return the way you came, turn left or north toward North Light, or right and south, toward Mansion Beach.

All of Clay Head is a hot spot for migratory birds in the spring and fall because it provides their two main requirements: ponds to drink from and many types of food to eat, from insects to fruiting shrubs. They especially like the numerous shrub-covered ponds because there is protection from migrating raptors, which feed on smaller birds that are worn out from the exertion of their migration.

Though many of the Japanese black pine trees here have died—victims of the turpentine beetle—the dead trees provide homes for insects that provide food for migratory songbirds intent on storing up fuel for their long flights north or south. One of the prime places for songbird observation is at the extreme north end of the trail, to the west of where the path meets the dirt lane. The Nature Conservancy and the U.S. Fish & Wildlife Service preserved this property in 1999. The parcel was a priority for conservation because it is at the northernmost extent of the Island and is a launching pad for migratory birds that orient north before their migration.

VIEWS There are many fine views from the walking trails on Block Island, but none are finer than the vistas along the Clay Head Trail. To the south is the village and Old Harbor Point. You can even see the top of the Southeast Light in the distance. Looking west from the southern part of the trail, there are views of Beacon Hill and beyond. The northern part of the path hugs the bluff closely in many places, and there are incredible views of the ocean. The Rhode Island shore is in the distance, and on clear days the Newport Bridge (the Pell Bridge between Newport and Jamestown) is visible. At the northern end of the trail, on the rise before it begins its descent, look to the northwest for Sachem Pond, the North Light, and the National Wildlife Refuge along West Beach.

The Long Lot Trail has a wonderful enclosed feeling running through thick vegetation interspersed by small open meadows and a number of isolated ponds. There are some high points, however, which offer commanding views of Great Salt Pond, Beacon Hill, Crescent Beach and the village in the far distance.

NATURAL AND HISTORIC FEATURES This is the first large area on the Island to be preserved and opened to the public, which was possible through the generosity of the Lapham Family. This area was meadow when the Laphams purchased it in the 1950s, but it is now coastal shrub, which is optimal habitat for bird life, especially migrants. The trees here are what remain of the 20,000 planted by Elise and David Lapham as part of their measures to enhance the property for wildlife. The Laphams have been banding birds here every spring and fall since 1967, which makes it one of the longest continuous monitoring projects on the East Coast. Many prominent ornithologists have done research here, and in 2001 the American Birds Conservancy named Block Island a globally important bird area.

6

The distinctive 80-foot high bluffs are the first glimpse of the Island for those arriving by ferry from Point Judith. We can thank the Laphams for the fact that most people's initial view is of unspoiled hills, an open landscape still reminiscent of the island that the Native Americans and European settlers discovered upon their arrival. These same bluffs are also home to the state-endangered barn owl, which builds its nest toward the top of the bluff, just under the vegetation. There are approximately four nests on the Island, the only place in Rhode Island where this species of owl can be found reproducing. This is yet another example of how Block Island has become an offshore refuge for species that have disappeared elsewhere in the region.

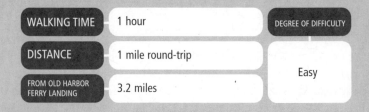

WALKING TIME	1 hour
DISTANCE	1 mile round-trip
FROM OLD HARBOR FERRY LANDING	3.2 miles

DEGREE OF DIFFICULTY

Easy

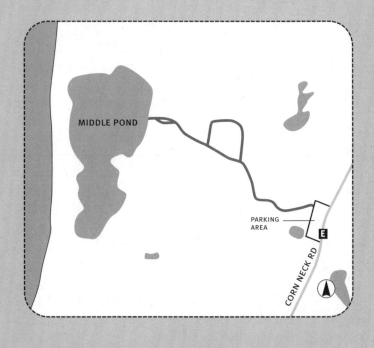

MIDDLE POND

PARKING AREA

CORN NECK RD

E

———— Roadways

———— Trail

———— Coastal Features

■ E Trail Entrance

| 0 | 0.25 | 0.50 | 0.75 |

HODGE FAMILY WILDLIFE PRESERVE

LOCATION This preserve is one-quarter of a mile north of the Clay Head Preserve entrance directly off Corn Neck Road. Look for the parking lot outlined in split-rail fencing. The parking lot entrance is through a stonewall gap marked by a wooden post on either side.

HISTORY OF TRAIL For more than 20 years, the Hodge Property was a priority for conservation groups on Block Island. Finally in December 2002 the Block Island Land Trust, Block Island Conservancy, Town of New Shoreham and The Nature Conservancy purchased it from members of the Hodge Family. Conservation staff and volunteers constructed the trail and parking lot in March of 2003, and the Hodge Family Wildlife Preserve was dedicated in May of 2004.

DESCRIPTION OF TRAIL This trail proceeds directly from the grass parking lot into a large meadow that is mowed annually in the spring and then is alive with wildflowers thereafter. It is a wonderful place to come at any time, but especially in the spring at dusk to watch the ritual display of the American woodcock.

This plump 11-inch bird has bulging eyes and a long bill, making it one of the strangest looking animals on the Island. With its wings whistling, the male flies in widening spirals rising up to 100 feet, circling at the highest point, and then abruptly zigzagging to earth like a falling leaf. When he reaches the ground, he releases a nasal sounding "peent." He then begins the process again; it is a display that is repeated many times in succession.

When you reach the former house site situated next to a tall tree, there is a superb vantage point for observing the conserved land that continues from there to the North Light in the distance. Continuing on, the trail turns west (left) through a coastal shrub habitat important for

9

Merlin

migrating songbirds and raptors. When the trail reaches a spur, we recommend the right-hand route because it affords some of the most spectacular views on Block Island. While walking through the meadows, watch for milkweed in the highest density found on the Island. Upon reaching the stonewall, the trail turns again to the west (left) and follows the stonewall boundary of the Breed Land, one of the first gifts to conservation in 1972.

The spur trail eventually connects to the main trail and the opportunity to turn back east (left) to the parking lot or proceeding right (west) and a continuation of the walk. The extra effort is well worth it as the trail ends at Middle Pond, which is strikingly beautiful in its own right and also a great spot to see egrets, herons and bitterns in the spring and fall.

It is also a wonderful destination in winter as this coastal pond provides shelter for wildlife from the ocean beyond the western dunes. On the way to Middle Pond, you may note houses for eastern bluebirds built by Island resident George Dodge. While this species does not currently nest on the Island, the hope is these boxes will inspire them to do so in the future.

One of the nice aspects of this walk is the ability to take spur trails that make it possible to traverse different ground going and returning. If you desire a longer walk after arriving back at the parking lot, just walk out to Corn Neck Road and proceed south (right) for 150 feet where you will find the entrance to the Long Lot Trail, described separately in the Clay Head section of this guide.

VIEWS If you never left your car upon arriving in the parking lot, the reason why this property was so important for conservation would be readily apparent. There is hardly a place on the property where there is not an exceptional view. This is an especially beautiful hike at sunset because of the way the light unfolds across the landscape. From this preserve, you can see towards the north the U. S. Fish & Wildlife Service's National Wildlife Refuge along the West Beach, Sachem Pond, Cow Cove, North Light and Middle Pond, one of the most pristine examples of a coastal salt pond remaining in Rhode Island. Straight across Block Island Sound is mainland Rhode Island, and to the west, Connecticut.

NATURAL AND HISTORIC FEATURES One of the reasons this property was so desirable for conservation is because more than 150 acres of preserved land abut it, running unobstructed to the ocean. All of this is visible from the parking lot and one of the Island's main roads. When pausing at the former house site, you can see across the fields towards the northeast to a house that is attached to a concrete observation bunker used to search for German U-boats during World War II. These virtually indestructible towers were scattered all around the Island during the war; the few that remain are incorporated into houses, like the one here. Many of the historic houses in the area represent different styles of East Coast architecture, from simple "Capes" to elegant Victorian cottages and "story and a half" farmhouses.

10

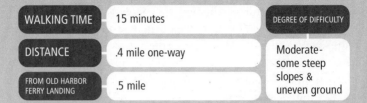

WALKING TIME	15 minutes	DEGREE OF DIFFICULTY
DISTANCE	.4 mile one-way	Moderate-some steep slopes & uneven ground
FROM OLD HARBOR FERRY LANDING	.5 mile	

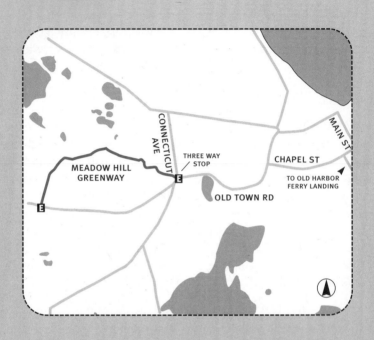

CONNECTICUT AVE

THREE WAY STOP

MEADOW HILL GREENWAY

CHAPEL ST

MAIN ST

TO OLD HARBOR FERRY LANDING

OLD TOWN RD

Roadways

Trail

Coastal Features

E Trail Entrance

0   0.25

MEADOW HILL GREENWAY

LOCATION There are two places to access this trail. There is an entrance by the stop sign at the intersection of Connecticut Avenue and Old Town Road; a more formal access point exists a third of a mile further west on Old Town Road, which is indicated by a granite "Greenway" marker.

HISTORY OF TRAIL This trail was made possible through the generosity of Merchant Marine Captain John R. and Alyce Lewis, who beginning in 1946 lived in the house on the hill that is encircled by the trail. They gave the surrounding five-acre parcel to the Block Island Conservancy in 1993, just another example of the many contributions the Lewis Family has made to conservation on Block Island. Captain Lewis was the first president of the Block Island Conservancy and a major part of the successful campaign to move the Southeast Lighthouse.

DESCRIPTION OF TRAIL This is the Greenway nearest to town, but it provides the opportunity for a short walk to a quiet place that seems further away from things than it is. This nearly half-mile route can be accessed at either its eastern or western end and makes a nice walk in itself, or it can be part of a larger hike. In fact, it makes a nice round trip for someone looking to get away from the activity of the Old Harbor for a bit. You can make an easy loop by entering at the Connecticut Avenue entrance, following the path until it ends, and then returning to the village by way of Old Town Road.

Due to the many different types of habitat in one small place, this is a great spot to look for birds, plants, and insects. Part of the walk is through meadows filled with wildflowers, such as milkweed, asters, and daisies. There is an extensive cattail marsh with a small fern-covered creek. Some of the Island's largest shadbushes, which are big enough to appear like trees (thought to be some of the tallest of this species in the

13

Yellow-bellied Sapsucker

world), can be found on the southern end of the trail. Keep your eyes open for the occasional apple tree, a magnet for many types of birds, such as warblers and woodpeckers.

VIEWS This trail has far more extensive views than are apparent from the road. In the distance, one can see Clay Head, Great Salt Pond, and the beaches to the east. Closer to the path, there are nice panoramas of cattail marshes, and the shadbushes and apple trees are spectacular when they flower in bright whites in early May.

NATURAL AND HISTORIC FEATURES Meadow Hill is a drumlin, formed by the glaciers. The walkway provides the opportunity to view some of the Island's most beautiful architecture, as well as natural scenery. The distinctive Block Island buildings one can see include old hotels and rooming houses such as the Highview Inn, Breakers, and Hygeia House. You can see the stark white, flat-roofed Georgian Weather Bureau above the Great Salt Pond. From 1887 to the 1930s observers recorded weather data for forecasters in the U.S. Weather Bureau.

The Meadow Hill Greenway trail passes through an avenue of shadbushes.

Roadways

Trail

Coastal Features

0   0.25   0.50   0.75   1

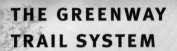

THE GREENWAY
TRAIL SYSTEM

The Greenway trail system is comprised of walks numbered four through nine. The Greenway runs east to west and north to south. The continuous system of trails makes it possible to walk from place to place from the shores of the Great Salt Pond in the north to the sea at Black Rock in the south and cross over only two paved roads and two dirt roads. Along the way are lots of side trails going towards the east and the west.

For ambitious hikers, walking the entire Greenway is well worth the effort. For those who prefer a more leisurely pace, pick out one section at a time and savor the experience. What follows are descriptions of the individual sections that comprise the Greenway and information and maps that illustrate how the segments interconnect to form a total of about 13 miles of walkways.

WALKING TIME	45 minutes one-way	**DEGREE OF DIFFICULTY**
DISTANCE	1 mile one-way	Moderate- some steep slopes & uneven ground
FROM OLD HARBOR FERRY LANDING	1.5 miles to north entrance 1.7 miles to south entrance	

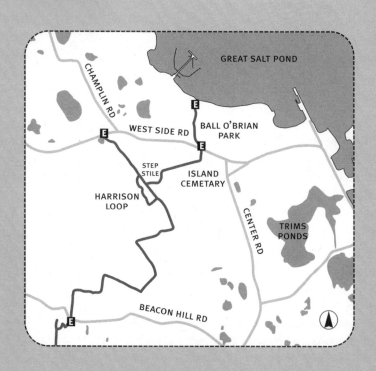

GREAT SALT POND

CHAMPLIN RD

WEST SIDE RD

BALL O'BRIAN PARK

STEP STILE

ISLAND CEMETARY

HARRISON LOOP

CENTER RD

TRIMS PONDS

BEACON HILL RD

E Trail Entrance

Roadways

Trail

Coastal Features

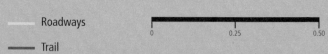

0   0.25   0.50

4

GREAT SALT POND TO
BEACON HILL ROAD LINK

LOCATION This is the northern end of the Greenway trail system, and there are two entrance points. The first is by the granite "Greenway" marker on West Side Road, nearly opposite the end of Champlin Road. It is also possible to begin at the Ball-O'Brien Park (opposite the main entrance to the Island Cemetery), then cross West Side Road and enter the cemetery and access the trail in the southwest corner of the cemetery. The path extends to the approximate halfway point of Beacon Hill Road, directly across from the entrance to the South Beacon/Nathan Mott Park trail, the access point for those who wish to continue further south along the Greenway.

HISTORY OF TRAIL This was the final major addition to the Greenway trail system. There were a number of people involved in conservation who wanted to create a path that would link the waters of Great Salt Pond with the bluffs at Black Rock. This was made possible in the fall of 1998—thanks to the generosity of landowners in this area of Beacon Hill —and opened for walking the following spring. The Beacon Hill Homeowners Association and the Erlanger, Tonner, and Harrison families all granted walking easements over their properties. When Christopher Walling sold a key parcel to the Block Island Conservancy at a bargain price, the path system was complete.

DESCRIPTION OF TRAIL There are two ways to start this walk. The trail begins off West Side Road at the "Greenway" marker near the end of Champlin Road. You can start at this point and take in the Harrison Loop or, if you prefer, begin at the Ball-O'Brien Property by the shore of Great Salt Pond and proceed up the hill into the Island Cemetery. Just past the top of the rise, take the first right and proceed west to the corner of the cemetery where there are wooden steps, called a "stile," over the stonewall to the trail on the other side. The path to the left then follows the undulating hills, crossing stonewalls at different points and eventually reaching Beacon Hill Road, where you can continue on across the lane to Nathan Mott Park and Turnip Farm or retrace your steps back to New Harbor.

This trail provides a winding journey through the center of the Island, a relatively remote area where few people travel — even in the summer months. The landscape is thickly covered with mature shrubs and trees, and there are many places where the vegetation joins to create a canopy above your head. It is possible to forget you are on Block Island as you pass through an enclosed area where the brush is dense and impenetrable, and the light is filtered through overhanging leaves and branches.

19

The wildlife abounds in this environment, and it is common to see white-tailed deer and many different species of birds. Common nesting birds include the gray catbird, yellow warbler, Carolina wren, song sparrow, and common yellowthroat. Ring-necked pheasant, which were introduced to the Island, are common here and can bring you abruptly out of your reverie if you flush one and experience the ruckus they make upon being disturbed. The young of these beautiful birds are a common source of food for the American burying beetle. This federally endangered insect is discussed in detail in the Rodman's Hollow/Black Rock section of the guide.

Song Sparrow

Watch for the rare golden-winged warbler in the spring and fall. Listen also for the eastern towhees in the summer; their song sounds as if they are singing, "Drink your tea." In the winter, one can often hear the white-throated sparrows whistling, "Poor old Sam Peabody, Peabody." It is possible to see great flocks of birds in this part of the Island at any time of year.

VIEWS While the vegetation prevents the wide views that are common in many other areas of the trail system, there are still nice vistas to be found on this path. At different points, the landscape opens up, making it possible to see glimpses of town, New Harbor, and Clay Head. The Ball-O'Brien Property is the only conservation area on this part of the Great Salt Pond and was protected by the Block Island Land Trust and the Town of New Shoreham to preserve access to the water for the public and have a playground and other recreation facilities. The hill in the center of the property provides a wonderful prospect of what is arguably the Island's foremost natural resource.

20

NATURAL AND HISTORIC FEATURES The distinctive features of this trail are the verdant vegetation and rolling hills. The habitats found on this walk are different than any other trail on the Island. In the summer, there are places where the thick vegetation and cacophony of wildlife sounds create an almost jungle-like feel.

The Island Cemetery is the main burial place on Block Island. There are a number of distinctive headstones, particularly in the old part of the cemetery, which can be found on the hill above West Side and Center Roads. The view from here is one of the finest on the Island, providing a wonderful prospect of Great Salt Pond, Crescent Beach, and the Atlantic Ocean.

WALKING TIME	1.5 hours one-way	DEGREE OF DIFFICULTY
DISTANCE	1.33 miles one-way	Hard-steep slopes & uneven ground
FROM OLD HARBOR FERRY LANDING	1.7 miles to South Beacon Hill entrance, 1.5 miles to Nathan Mott Park entrance	

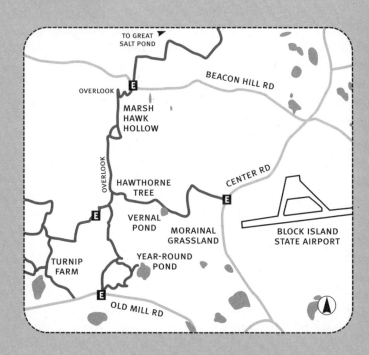

TO GREAT SALT POND

BEACON HILL RD

OVERLOOK

MARSH HAWK HOLLOW

OVERLOOK

HAWTHORNE TREE

CENTER RD

E

VERNAL POND

MORAINAL GRASSLAND

BLOCK ISLAND STATE AIRPORT

TURNIP FARM

YEAR-ROUND POND

E

OLD MILL RD

— Roadways

— Trail

— Coastal Features

E Trail Entrance

| 0 | 0.25 | 0.50 | 0.75 | 1 |

5

SOUTH BEACON HILL
& NATHAN MOTT PARK

LOCATION There are four different places to access Nathan Mott Park. The north-south Greenway trail goes through the park, beginning at the midpoint of Beacon Hill Road, continuing south, and then connecting to Turnip Farm. In the east, opposite the airport runway, there is an entrance with a parking area and bike rack. You can also enter or exit off Old Mill Road, about a third of a mile from Smilin' Thru or the eastern end of that road.

HISTORY OF TRAIL The portion of the trail from Beacon Hill Road to Nathan Mott Park—once known as the Enchanted Forest—runs through property protected in 1991 through the generosity of Hal Oppenheimer and the Jules and Doris Stein Foundation. This part of the preserve is dedicated to the memory of Sally Hamilton Oppenheimer and Anne F. H. duPont. It is called Marsh Hawk Hollow. One of these magnificent birds was observed nesting there in 2005.

Nathan Mott Park was once the farm of Nathan Mott, who left it to his daughter Lucretia Mott Ball. His farm included the western half of what is now the Block Island State Airport; his barn once stood where the western end of the runway is now. Upon Lucretia Mott Ball's death in 1941, the property was left to the Nathan Mott Park Corporation, thereby beginning the land-conservation movement on Block Island. In the early 1940s, Earl Dodge, a Block Island naturalist, led the effort to plant the forest with the help of Island high school students. In 1996, Nathan Mott Park trustees transferred ownership to the Block Island Conservancy with a management easement to The Nature Conservancy. Here you will find not a refined urban park with amenities but a natural preserve pretty much untouched by human changes.

DESCRIPTION OF TRAIL Nathan Mott Park is a destination in itself, part of the main north-south Greenway trail system. There is a path entering from the east by the airport, which provides a good place to park or leave a bike. The trail from the east and the main Greenway trail connect at the top of a steep hill, made easier to traverse by a set of steps built into it. The steps also help to control erosion. To the north, the trail leads out to Beacon Hill Road, where it joins the North Beacon trail directly across the road. Off this path there are two spurs, one that leads to an overlook providing views to the east all the way to Old Harbor and another that goes down an old cart way bounded by stonewalls.

23 From the spot where the east and main trail connect, if you follow the trail to the south, you will soon come to another junction. By going right or to the west, you connect to Turnip Farm and the continuation of the Greenway. The path to the left goes east through what was once the Enchanted Forest but the southern half of it was cleared in 2004 and returned to meadow habitat because the Federal Aviation Administration deemed the trees to be obstructions to airplanes taking off and landing at the Block Island State Airport. There is a pleasant loop to this trail that takes you down to a year-round pond that is home to the damselfly, lilypad forktail, northern water snake, and eastern painted turtle. This path ends at Old Mill Road, where, at some point in the near future, it will connect across the lane to a new link trail to Rodman's Hollow.

In this 46-acre preserve lie most of the main habitats found on Block Island. There is meadow that is managed by mowing every few years to provide a home for the Block Island meadow vole and many species of wildflowers. A small stand of exotic trees is host to one of the only fish crow nests on the Island. A fish crow looks the same as an American crow, but it's smaller with a more nasal sounding call.

A vernal pond can also be found here. Vernal ponds dry up in the summer. While they do not have fish, there are generally red-spotted newts, which are salamanders, and spring peepers, which are tree frogs, and a wide variety of aquatic insects. There is a year-round pond that in the past has supported the Island's only wood duck nest. The prevalent coastal shrub provides great cover and berries for migratory songbirds. Many state-endangered flowers and plants occur in areas of morainal grassland, a globally imperiled community type, found near the Nathan Mott Park entrance. Morainal grasslands are an ecological community of plants found throughout the southwest part of Block Island in sparse, sandy to gravelly soils on hillsides or hilltops.

When entering the park from the east, you enter a meadow that was opened up as part of the airport obstruction project. At this point, listen for the "Drink your tea" call of the eastern towhee and the "Witchety, witchety, witchety" of the common yellowthroat. The trail proceeds through some heavy shrub before opening up into another meadow where you will see climbing vines with hanging seedpods; this is the black swallowwort, an extremely invasive plant in the milkweed family. To your left (south) is a morainal grassland where you may notice the soil is sparse, very sandy, and not hospitable to shrubs. As you head up the hill, there is a vernal pond that is home to a giant diving beetle, found in New England only on Block Island. The first big tree you come to on your right is a hawthorn. The thorns of the sweet green briar that follow protect nesting gray catbirds from predators.

24

At the base of the hill, you come upon the stairs that lead up the hill. To your right, is an area that was infected by the turpentine beetle, the insect responsible for the demise of Japanese black pines here and throughout the Island. Most of the forest, which also sustained heavy damage from Hurricane Bob and the Perfect Storm of October 1991, was cut down and returned to meadow in 2004 during the airport project. This area now features excellent views of the village to the east and the entire southeastern part of the Island, including the top of the Southeast Light turret in the far distance. The northern part of the Enchanted Forest remains and the Chinese chestnut and sycamore maple can still be found there.

VIEWS This area is one of the highest spots on Block Island. The preserve also offers intriguing inland views of shrubs, ponds, and a small, glacially formed hollow.

NATURAL AND HISTORIC FEATURES This is the first park on Block Island, an area set aside expressly for the enjoyment of the public by an incredibly foresighted woman, Lucretia Mott Ball. She is also known for her generous donation of the Adrian House—a former hotel that is now home to the Harbor Baptist Church—and items of her personal property that helped inspire the creation of the Block Island Historical Society.

There are two benches in the park, which Block Island High School students made in 1998 to provide rest for weary hikers. The sign located at the entrance of the Nathan Mott Park trail, painted by Island artist Cindy Kelly, is based on the original.

This is a great walk for those who want to learn about the natural history of Block Island. For a more in-depth study of Nathan Mott Park, self-guided walk pamphlets are available at the kiosk at the eastern entrance and at The Nature Conservancy office on High Street.

WALKING TIME	2 hours one-way
DISTANCE	1.7 miles one-way
FROM OLD HARBOR FERRY LANDING	2.5 miles

DEGREE OF DIFFICULTY

Easy/moderate- a few steep slopes

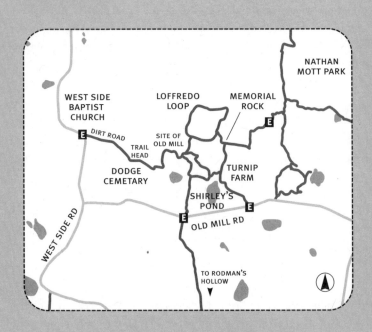

Roadways

Trail

Coastal Features

 Trail Entrance

TURNIP FARM & ELAINE LOFFREDO PRESERVE TRAILS

LOCATION As in Nathan Mott Park, there are four ways to enter and exit Turnip Farm and Loffredo Preserve. The main Greenway trail comes in from Nathan Mott Park, winds through the farm, and then joins the path to Rodman's Hollow on Old Mill Road, three-tenths of a mile from the West Side Road end.

At about the midpoint of Old Mill Road is the main Turnip Farm entrance, where there is a parking area and a bike rack. To enter Turnip Farm from the west, look for the dirt lane at the bend of West Side Road east of the former West Side Baptist Church that is marked by a large rock with the words "Dodge Cemetery" engraved on it. Follow that lane to Dodge Cemetery and look for the turnstile leading to the trails.

HISTORY OF TRAIL Turnip Farm was the first purchase of the Block Island Land Trust in 1987. The farm was preserved with the generous help of its owners, Burt and Melanie King, for passive recreation and protection of wildlife habitat.

Elaine Loffredo Preserve was protected by The Nature Conservancy with the help of Robert Loffredo and neighboring landowners. This land is preserved in remembrance of his wife, Elaine, whose life was tragically cut short in the crash of TWA Flight 800 off Long Island, New York, on July 17, 1996.

Other properties in this part of the preserve include Shirley's Pond, dedicated to the memory of Shirley Wood, who together with her husband, Peter, donated the pond and land surrounding it to The Nature Conservancy. This is the site of the annual ecumenical service sponsored in August by conservation groups. Further to the west are properties protected to expand Turnip Farm Preserve and connect it to the historic, town-owned Dodge Cemetery. There is also a walking easement generously donated by Dan and Jean Larkin, which provides a vital connection in the Greenway trail system.

DESCRIPTION OF TRAIL The Greenway trail enters Turnip Farm from the north at the boundary with Nathan Mott Park. As it winds through the farm, it runs primarily east to west. Look for signs where paths intersect with the main trail.

One path connects to the main Turnip Farm entrance, which is the best place to park or leave a bike in this area of the Greenway. Another spur goes west into Loffredo Preserve where it comes back on itself or joins a path to the west and the trail to Dodge Cemetery. Further west along the main trail, there is an intersection by a small, wooden bridge. To the south is the through trail to Rodman's Hollow. If you continue west at this point, the path leads out to West Side Road or connects to Loffredo Preserve and makes a circuit back through Turnip Farm.

If you enter from Old Mill Road using the Turnip Farm entrance, look for the sandy soil, which provides ideal habitat for many types of wildflowers. Look for many small yellow flowers with hairy leaves: the mouse-ear hawkweed, which blooms in June. That is also the time of year to find another yellow flower: the bushy rockrose. The state-endangered northern blazing star, a spiked purple plant, blooms here in the fall. The domestic version of this plant, the gayfeather, can be found in many gardens. Autumn also finds migrating monarch butterflies filling the open fields by the trail's edge.

On Loffredo Preserve, the land climbs higher and you will come to a memorial stone, which sets the tone nicely for this part of the trail. The vegetation here is rich with black cherry, bayberry, and shadbush. Listen for the "Chickadee, dee, dee, dee" of the black-capped chickadee, and keep an eye out for owl pellets, regurgitated fur, and bones left by barn owls, which hunt in the vicinity. Other raptors can also often be seen overhead looking for prey. When the berries are ripe in the fall, this is an excellent spot to go birdwatching.

At Shirley's Pond, the sound of green frogs calling can be heard in the summer. There are also large dragonflies on the prowl called common green darners. This beautiful pond is a good spot to see the American black duck and wading birds, such as the green heron and great blue heron. In the winter, it is outlined in black alder or winterberry, a shrub in the holly family. The bright red berries are a very important food source for wintering birds, especially ring-necked pheasants, during the cold weather months.

The trail to the west passes by the site of an old sail-powered windmill, which gives the nearby dirt road its name. The mill's foundation can be seen from the trail during the times of year when the vegetation thins. The trail ends at Dodge Cemetery, then the walk continues along the dirt road that connects to West Side Road, near the former West Side Baptist Church. Dodge Cemetery is an excellent example of the numerous small cemeteries on the Island, which harken back to the time when families were born, lived, and buried in the same area of the Island.

VIEWS The upper part of Turnip Farm is among the highest points on Block Island. As a result, there are wonderful views from the trails on the farm and the Loffredo Loop. To the south is Shirley's Pond with the fields of Lewis Farm in the distance. Looking to the west, one can see Long Island Sound and, on clear days, Montauk Point at the tip of Long Island. It is a great spot to watch the sunset. The higher elevations also provide a wonderful prospect for seeing the preserve. This, combined with Nathan Mott Park, is one of the largest preserved areas, and it is possible to get a sense of the openness that was once common through-out the Island.

NATURAL AND HISTORIC FEATURES The rolling hills here are clear evidence of the glacial formation of this area of the Island. The open fields of Turnip Farm, which are mowed regularly, look much as they have for generations. There are numerous, globally imperiled morainal grasslands on the farm, mostly concentrated near the Old Mill Road entrance. Enclosures are erected there frequently to protect rare plants, such as the northern blazing star and purple needlegrass, from the deer. If these species of plants are not enclosed, they can be damaged by the browsing of deer.

Dodge Cemetery, at the western end of the preserve, contains the grave of a veteran of the Civil War. Though the cemetery is named for a member of the Dodge Family, the majority of those buried here were Roses, another family of the earliest white settlers, who made their homes on the West Side. The mill, which once existed on the hill to the east of Dodge Cemetery, operated in the Nineteenth Century to grind the grain from neighboring farms.

WALKING TIME	2 hours one-way
DEGREE OF DIFFICULTY	
DISTANCE	2.6 miles one-way
FROM OLD HARBOR FERRY LANDING	2.8 miles

Moderate-steep slopes & uneven ground

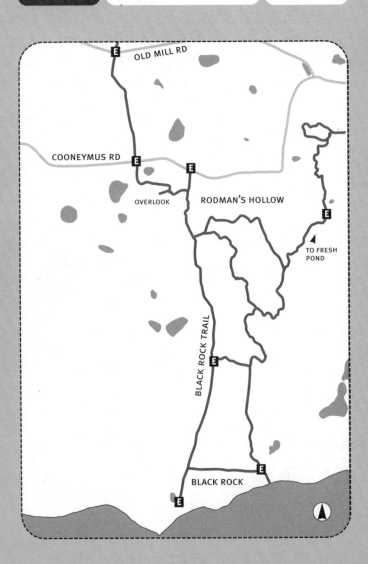

OLD MILL RD

COONEYMUS RD

OVERLOOK

RODMAN'S HOLLOW

TO FRESH POND

BLACK ROCK TRAIL

BLACK ROCK

Roadways

Trail

Coastal Features

 Trail Entrance

0   0.25   0.50   0.75   1

OLD MILL ROAD & COONEYMUS ROAD LINK TO RODMAN'S HOLLOW & BLACK ROCK TRAILS

LOCATION The Greenway link trail can be found on Old Mill Road, about three-tenths of a mile from West Side Road. The entrance is directly across the road from the path connecting to the main trail north into Turnip Farm and onto Nathan Mott Park. The other end of the link is on Cooneymus Road, slightly west of the road to Black Rock and directly across the paved road from the trail leading into Rodman's Hollow Preserve. (When walking on Black Rock Road, keep an eye open for bikes and horses.) Read the trail description that follows to discover how the Rodman's Hollow trail connects to the Greenway trail running east to Fresh Pond.

HISTORY OF TRAIL When the idea to connect large conservation areas by walking trails was conceived, it became apparent that the effort could be possible only if private landowners would grant easements over their property. An easement in this context allows the public to walk on a certain part of your property without relinquishing ownership. This is a common practice in England but not in the United States. Fortunately, Peter and Shirley Wood volunteered to open a path through their land, and the Guerry and Asch families agreed to participate as well.

Their generosity made it possible to create a continuous system that brought together the conservation lands surrounding Rodman's Hollow with Turnip Farm Preserve. New trails were then created through the hollow, and the current integrated system was complete. These paths were opened to hikers in 1989. The name *Greenway* was inspired by the English conservation tradition of greenbelts between populated areas.

DESCRIPTION OF TRAIL The Greenway link continues the main north-south trail, which begins at Great Salt Pond and connects to Rodman's Hollow Preserve. The Rodman's Hollow section begins on the south side of Cooneymus Road. As this path winds up a hill, vast views open toward the ocean can be seen. Then the path descends to merge with Black Rock Road, an unpaved road.

Go right or south at this point and proceed until you see the fence and turnstile denoting the entrance into the trails. Shortly after entering, the path diverges. Regardless of whether you choose to go to the right or left at the fork, keep in mind that the two branches will eventually reunite before splitting again with connections back to Black Rock Road or a new path leading directly south to the bluff.

If you go left, the path proceeds through the bottom of the Hollow where you can study the deep ravine cut by glaciers through the land-scape. It also connects to the Peckham Farm/Fresh Pond Trail for those who want to continue their hike to the east. This trail appears on your left and leads up a steep slope to Peckham Farm. If you continue straight at this juncture, the trail angles to the west, climbs a ridge, and merges with the other branch of the original trail.

If you go to the right at the fork, the path follows the ridge that runs above the Hollow. Here are numerous places to stop and enjoy the view. When the trails converge, the path proceeds south to a hilltop with a fantastic vantage point over this entire area of the Island. To the east are open meadows and farm fields; the view to the south is of heavy brush and trees running to the bluff at the ocean's edge; undulating hills with a mosaic of vegetations lie to the west where you can see Lewis Farm on the distant horizon. The prospect north extends inland over the Hollow to Turnip Farm and beyond.

Just past the hilltop, the trail splits again. If you stay right and proceed directly west, you will arrive back on Black Rock Road where you can go left to the beach at Black Rock, or right, and follow the winding lane back to Cooneymus Road.

To the left at this point is a new path, opened in early 2006, that was made possible by the acquisition of the Jones Property by The Nature Conservancy and Block Island Land Trust in December of 2005. If you choose this route, which we highly recommend, it is immediately apparent why this property had long been a priority for conservation and is now a critical addition to the preserve that previously surrounded it.

The new path proceeds through stands of black locus, black gum, beech, ginkgo and pin oak planted in 1966 under the direction of Walter Jones.

The newly acquired Jones Property

At some point, part of the property will be cleared to benefit grassland species while leaving certain specimen trees to enhance and diversify the landscape. There are wonderful views along the way with the most spectacular of all awaiting you when the trail ends in a small grove of trees on a high bluff overlooking the ocean at Black Rock. From this vantage point, you will only see the Black Rock during an extreme low tide. This landmark for boaters and fishermen is submerged off the beach.

In the spring and fall, Rodman's Hollow is a good place to see migrating raptors riding the winds as they soar above the Hollow. In the grassy areas, look for savannah sparrows, ring-necked pheasants, and northern harriers. Because there are no ground predators on Block Island, the state-endangered harrier is successful at nesting, and there are believed to be as many as ten nests on the Island. The hollow is a popular hunting ground for this raptor, and it is common to see this beautiful bird, with its distinctive white rump, swooping over the fields after its prey of voles, snakes, or mice. In the spring, it is possible to see the loping sky dance, a mating ritual of the gray-backed male.

American Burying Beetle

Rodman's Hollow Preserve is managed primarily in meadow habitat for the benefit of the federally endangered American burying beetle. Block Island has the only natural population of this species east of the Mississippi River. The burying beetle, which can measure up to one and a quarter inches long, is black with orange markings. They are nocturnal, spending their nights searching for carrion. Once they find a dead animal, they bury it and create a cavern for the female to lay her eggs. The larvae then are raised, eating the carrion until they become adults and strike out on their own. For insects, the beetles display an unusual degree of parental care.

There are numerous theories as to why the American burying beetle has survived on Block Island. There is less outdoor lighting to attract them at night and deter them from searching for carrion; there are no mammals, such as raccoons, fox, or coyotes, to compete with them for carrion; and the Island has large open fields to provide appropriate habitat. Also, Block Island has never been sprayed with pesticides in a wholesale fashion, unlike many other places in the eastern United States.

Here are also several globally imperiled morainal grasslands, similar to those found on Turnip Farm. The pond, which lies to the west of Black Rock Road and is visible from the ridge trail, has no fish but does have green frogs and insect larvae. This pond can completely disappear during dry summers. In May, the shadbushes bloom white, and there is no better place on Block Island to observe their beauty than the overlook above Rodman's Hollow. These shrubs acquired their name because they bloom at the same time of year that a species of fish called shad begins their spawning runs.

34

VIEWS In many places, the trail runs along ridges and therefore offers expansive views in all directions. Unlike other areas of the Island where there are impediments in certain sight lines, here it is possible to see in all directions, especially to the open Atlantic Ocean to the south and southwest. These vistas encompass the preserve, with its mosaic of brush and meadow and unobstructed views of the open Atlantic to the south and southwest.

NATURAL AND HISTORIC FEATURES Rodman's Hollow is a glacial outwash channel. When the glacier started melting, sand and gravel were transported by the meltwater and created a broad plain to the north and east. The deep ravine, or hollow, that formed was cut by this same meltwater flowing over the sediments. Rodman's Hollow has a permeable layer that allows water to filter to the porous sediments below. As a result, water does not build up and form ponds, as it does at the nearby Fresh Pond and Peckham Pond.

This is the birthplace of the modern conservation era on Block Island. The Block Island Conservancy was founded in 1972 to protect Rodman's Hollow from imminent development and to preserve it for the benefit of the public. A sign that stands above the north end of the hollow at the overlook by Cooneymus Road commemorates this effort.

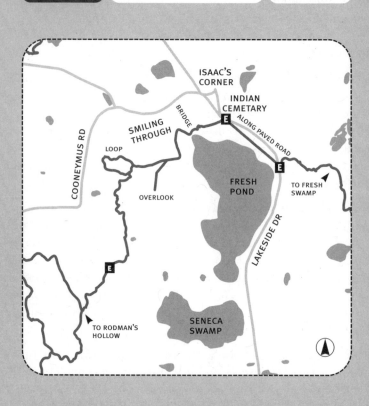

WALKING TIME	1 hour one-way
DISTANCE	.8 mile one-way
FROM OLD HARBOR FERRY LANDING	2 miles

DEGREE OF DIFFICULTY

Hard-steep slopes & uneven ground

ISAAC'S CORNER

INDIAN CEMETERY

BRIDGE

SMILING THROUGH

LOOP

COONEYMUS RD

OVERLOOK

ALONG PAVED ROAD

FRESH POND

TO FRESH SWAMP

LAKESIDE DR

TO RODMAN'S HOLLOW

SENECA SWAMP

—— Roadways

—— Trail

—— Coastal Features

E Trail Entrance

0	0.25	0.50	0.75	1

FRESH POND TRAIL

LOCATION The Fresh Pond trail has two access points. The main entrance is by a granite "Greenway" marker on Lakeside Drive, just south of where it intersects with Cooneymus Road. The other end of the path is on the ridge above Rodman's Hollow, where it merges with the Rodman's Hollow/Black Rock trail.

HISTORY OF TRAIL This trail came about because of the desire to extend the Greenway west to east, as well as north to south. It passes through two former farms. The easternmost section, or Smilin' Thru, runs through property protected in 1989 by the Block Island Land Trust with the help of a state open space grant. The Peckham Farm portion is the result of an agreement with the Peckham Farm Homeowners Association, who agreed to donate an easement and open the property to the public in exchange for help from Island conservation groups in purchasing undeveloped lots, thus reducing the density of the subdivision.

DESCRIPTION OF TRAIL The Fresh Pond trail is part of the Greenway trail system, connecting with the Fresh Swamp/Payne Farm trail on Lakeside Drive. There is a distance of two-tenths of a mile between the access points of the two paths, with the Fresh Pond trail lying to the north. Both entrances are clearly defined by granite "Greenway" markers by the side of the main road.

Beginning in the east, the Fresh Pond trail passes through open meadows and by the side of the pond, before it proceeds uphill toward the Peckham Farm neighborhood. There is a spur trail leading to an overlook on the way up to the ridge. Once in the Peckham Farm Homeowners Association subdivision, follow the granite markers until you reach the connecting point with the Rodman's Hollow trail and the continuation of the Greenway to the west.

The fields around Fresh Pond are a good place to look for raptors, such as the state-endangered northern harrier, best identified by the white patch on its rump. Vagrant bald eagles and nesting ospreys can also be seen in this area. In 2005, the first osprey nest was recorded on Block Island. It was on a platform at the Block Island Power Company and fledged one chick. By the pond shore, there is a bridge across a creek where green frogs can be found. Past the creek is a cove that is home to many dragonflies and eastern painted turtles. Listen to see whether you can hear the "Concurree" of the red-winged blackbird.

37

The trail passes through a succession of various shrubs; bayberry, arrow-wood, and shadbush are the most common. When you reach the hilltop, be sure to take the time to walk the spur trail and enjoy the pastoral view across open fields running to the pond shore. Just before the path begins its descent into Rodman's Hollow, note how gravelly the soil becomes in contrast to the verdant fields on the other side of the ridge. This is the edge of the glacial outwash or meltwater channel that formed the hollow.

VIEWS There are two spectacular views from this path. From the ridge looking east, one can see open fields that run down to the shores of Fresh Pond. On the trail's western end, there is a wonderful panorama across Rodman's Hollow. This is an excellent vantage point to see the beginning of the glacial formation as it begins its southerly run to the sea at Black Rock. In the distance to the west, the houses and barns of Lewis Farm are outlined on the horizon.

NATURAL AND HISTORIC FEATURES Fresh Pond is the deepest fresh-water pond on the Island and serves as a secondary reservoir for the town's water system. The Manisseans had camps here, and the first white settlers dug caves by the pond to live in temporarily until they could build more permanent structures.

Across the road from the trail entrance is Indian Cemetery. On the southwest corner of the intersection of Cooneymus Road and Lakeside Drive, known locally as Isaac's Corner, is the site of the home of Isaac Church, the last of the Manisseans, who died in 1886. From the trail-head, you can see a weathered, shingled gambrel-roofed cottage, which is a replica of the home of Arthur Penn, composer of the 1918 song "Smilin' Thru ," for which the house and this part of the trail are named.

Northern Arrowwood

WALKING TIME	1 hour one-way	DEGREE OF DIFFICULTY
DISTANCE	.9 mile one-way	Moderate-Fresh Swamp: steep slopes, Payne Farm: fields with stone walls to climb over
FROM OLD HARBOR FERRY LANDING	2.2 miles	

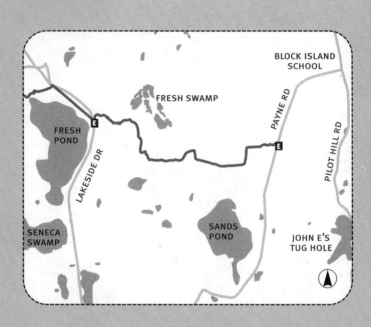

--- Roadways

— Trail

— Coastal Features

E Trail Entrance

0   0.25   0.50   0.75   1

FRESH SWAMP & PAYNE FARM TRAIL

LOCATION The eastern end of this trail is on Payne Road, four-tenths of a mile from where it intersects with High Street at the school. The western end is located on Lakeside Drive, a fifth of a mile south of the entrance to the Fresh Pond trail, near the Indian Cemetery at the intersection of Lakeside Drive and Cooneymus Road.

HISTORY OF TRAIL Payne Farm was once the largest farm on Block Island. Harriet Payne Phelan, a descendant of the Payne Family, along with her husband, Bill, generously sold—at below market value—the Fresh Swamp portion to The Nature Conservancy in 1991. This purchase was made possible by grants from the state of Rhode Island, The Champlin Foundations, and the Norcross Foundation.

The second phase of the preserve was completed in 1992 when The Nature Conservancy, together with the Block Island Land Trust, purchased an easement over the farm fields from Bill and Harriet's son, Blake, and his wife, Michele. This addition to Fresh Swamp Preserve created a contiguous band of protected land from Lakeside Drive to Payne Road. This critical acquisition made it possible to extend the Greenway trail system to the east from Smilin' Thru and Fresh Pond, and it afforded protection for the town's water supply.

DESCRIPTION OF TRAIL The Fresh Swamp/Payne Farm trail entrance on Payne Road marks the eastern end of the Greenway trail system; it is about 1.1 miles from the village in Old Harbor. The path crosses the fields of Payne Farm and then proceeds into heavy brush as it winds its way to Lakeside Drive by Fresh Pond. To connect to the Fresh Pond trail, take a right and walk a short distance along the side of the main road until you see the "Greenway" marker and the continuation of the path. The best place to park in this area of the Greenway is by the side of Lakeside Drive, as the only place to park on Payne Road is by the school.

There is an abrupt delineation between the two sections of this trail. While the Fresh Swamp portion runs through heavy growth, at times creating a tunnel-like effect, the Payne Farm part of the path proceeds through some of the largest open fields on Block Island. The meadows here are important for wildflowers like butterfly weed, asters, and hawkweed.

In the summer, over the meadows there are often swallows and dragonflies looking for mosquitoes and other small insects on which they prey. The big dragonflies are common green darners, and they migrate through Block Island in the spring and fall. This is also a good spot to see monarch butterflies in the autumn. The monarch caterpillars are found exclusively on common milkweed. Look for a white caterpillar with black and yellow spots eating the milkweed leaves. By eating the toxic milkweed, the monarchs take on a foul taste, thus making them unappetizing to birds. In the winter, listen and look for the large beautiful bird with a yellow breast: the eastern meadowlark.

The Fresh Swamp section is very heavily vegetated and covered with shrubs important to birds, deer, and other animals. The path runs primarily along the high ground on the southern portion of the property. The lower-lying land to the north contains a system of ponds and wetlands, which give this area its name.

A small bridge on the trail runs over a creek. This creek, in evidence only during wet periods, is one of the few aboveground streams on the Island. In this area, the birds are particularly active. Listen here for the song sparrow, two clear notes with a twirl, as well as the eastern towhee, gray catbird, and Carolina wren. You are in some of the richest moist shrub habitat on the Island.

VIEWS This is truly two paths in one. Fresh Swamp offers an enclosed feeling, with inland views across the preserve at different junctures. Where the paths converge, the landscape opens up to the east, and there are long views across open fields to the ocean and even to Clay Head in the distance.

NATURAL AND HISTORIC FEATURES At Payne Farm the hayed pastures and finely maintained farmhouse, built in 1877, offer the image of a historic farming landscape that is found now in few places on Block Island or the mainland beyond. These meadows and nearby wetlands provide habitat for many endangered species. This preserve is vital to nature-education programs because of its proximity to the Block Island School.

Common Aster

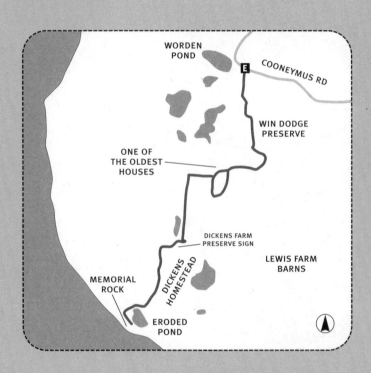

WALKING TIME	1.5 hours round-trip for Win Dodge & Dickens Farm combined	DEGREE OF DIFFICULTY
DISTANCE	2.36 miles round-trip for Win Dodge & Dickens Farm combined	Win Dodge: Hard-steep slopes & uneven ground, Dickens Farm: Easy
FROM OLD HARBOR FERRY LANDING	3.3 miles	

WORDEN POND

COONEYMUS RD

E

WIN DODGE PRESERVE

ONE OF THE OLDEST HOUSES

DICKENS FARM PRESERVE SIGN

LEWIS FARM BARNS

MEMORIAL ROCK

DICKENS HOMESTEAD

ERODED POND

——— Roadways

——— Trail

——— Coastal Features

E Trail Entrance

0   0.25   0.50   0.75   1

WIN DODGE & DICKENS FARM TRAILS

LOCATION Those who are familiar with the description of the trail in the first edition of the guide may want to pay particular attention to a number of changes that took place in this area in 2006. The Win Dodge and Dickens Farm Trails have become virtually one path leading to and from Dickens Point. The beginning of the trail can be accessed by way of Dickens Farm Road, an unmarked dirt lane off Cooneymus Road. Dickens Farm Road is slightly east and up the hill from Worden Pond, which lies next to the sharp bend where West Side and Cooneymus Roads intersect. If you are driving, it is best to leave your car along the main road or in the small parking lot next to the trail entrance.

Look for the "Walkers Welcome" sign on your left marking the beginning of the trail. The terrain is steep but before you exit on Dickens Farm Road you will be treated to sweeping views. At the dirt road, Dickens Farm Road, proceed left for less than a fifth of a mile until you come to the Dickens Farm Preserve sign announcing the start of that trail. This leads through open fields to the bluff above the Atlantic Ocean.

HISTORY OF TRAIL The Win Dodge Preserve is named in honor of Winfield Dodge, a previous owner of the property. This preserve was initiated by the Block Island Conservancy and added to adjoining conservation in the area starting in the mid-1990s. The ability to run the trail through conservation land and not along the road as before was made possible by the acquisition of a key connector parcel, the Soorikian Property, in 2004.

While the Win Dodge Trail is one of the newest on the Island, the Dickens Farm Trail it connects to is one of the oldest. The Dickens Family settled on Block Island in the late 1600s, and the Dickens homestead can still be seen from the trail. Miss Elizabeth Dickens, the "Bird Lady of Block Island" and a major influence on the conservation movement, was the last of the Dickens Family on the Island; she died here in 1963. In her life-time she was one of the nation's most renowned amateur ornithologists. William Lewis, of nearby Lewis Farm and a close friend of Miss Dickens, acquired the property from Miss Dickens's niece. In 1985 he sold most of the Dickens Farm to conservancy groups for less than market value, pre-serving that land forever.

The first path was cut at that time and dedicated to Bill's father, Clarence Lewis, the last person to farm the land, and Miss Dickens. Margaret Meiss, a New Jersey woman impressed by the conservation ethic on Block Island, made a major donation toward the "Preserve Like the Dickens" fund-raising effort. She is recognized for her generosity on the memorial rock that marks the end of the trail.

DESCRIPTION OF TRAIL The Win Dodge Trail commences with a steep climb through coastal shrub. The ascent is worth it, however, as there are memorable views of the area as you go. In the spring and summer, be sure to look for the northern harrier, which nests in the preserve. After a short distance, the hike continues through the Soorikian Property, whose critical location had made it a top priority for acquisition for more than 20 years. In addition to being a critical trail connector, this property is a mixture of shrubs and marsh that is extremely important nesting habitat for the Virginia rail and American woodcock. The trail loops through another Block Island Conservancy holding, the Lewis Ball tract, before exiting on Dickens Farm Road and the short walk along the lane to the Dickens Farm Preserve.

The Dickens Farm portion of the trail lies to the right of the road, immediately adjacent to the preserve sign. Follow the path through the fields down to the bluff where it ends at the memorial rock. After stop-ping to enjoy the view, retrace your steps back to Cooneymus Road.

VIEWS Because the Win Dodge Preserve is located on high ground, it offers wonderful vistas across the fields of Lewis Farm and Dickens Farm and Southwest Point. In the summer and fall, you will see large number of boats off shore drawn to this popular fishing spot by the prospect of catching stripped bass and bluefish. Listen for the sound of the sou'west buoy a few feet off the beach.

Dickens Farm, with its open fields and stonewalls, looks much the same as the entire Island did when it was heavily farmed from the time the early settlers cleared the forests until after World War II. From the bluff, the view is extremely rare on the East Coast of the United States because it looks west and south over open ocean.

A powerful hawk, the Harrier hunts over grassy fields and marshes and can often be seen hovering in the Win Dodge Preserve.

47

The entrance to Dickens Farm Trail

NATURAL AND HISTORIC FEATURES The many hills and kettle holes of the Win Dodge Preserve are the remnants of the glacial construction of the landscape in this area of the Island. Along the route, be on the lookout for symbols of the Island's agricultural past such as old barn foundations and stray apple trees.

Dickens Farm is now a managed grassland, which is mowed every two years. At the end of the trail, near the memorial rock, the vegetation changes and the land hollows out. This had been a pond until the dam on the bluff gave way in 1997 and the water drained out to the beach below.

The Dickens homestead is a wonderful example of early Island architecture. To the east, outlined against the sky, one can see the barns at Lewis Farm where Clarence Lewis once had his milking operation.

Please stay on the trail and do not get too close to the bluff or climb down it. Also, kindly respect the privacy of the owners of the Dickens homestead.

The Greenway Trail winding its way through Rodman's Hollow in the spring.

Littlefield Farm is an excellent example of the saltwater farms that once extended up and down the coast of the Island.

Some of the thousands of daffodils planted by the Lapham Family in the Clay Head Preserve.

This gapway connects two hayfields on the Island's west side.

These fields on the Lewis Dickens Farm Preserve are home to the highest percentage of endangered species in Rhode Island.

West side wall and meadow after a major winter snowstorm.

Ice boating on Sachem Pond.

Rodman's Hollow comes to life in springtime.

The newly cut hay will have to dry before it can be bailed.

The view across Clay Head Swamp to Littlefield Farm.

Georgian Swamp is resplendent with the colors of late fall.

The view across Champlin Farm to the Coast Guard station.

Hull Pond in springtime.

Gasner's Pond on a still summer morning.

The view down Crescent Beach toward Old Harbor.

North Light was built in 1867 and is the fourth lighthouse on this site.

Field notes

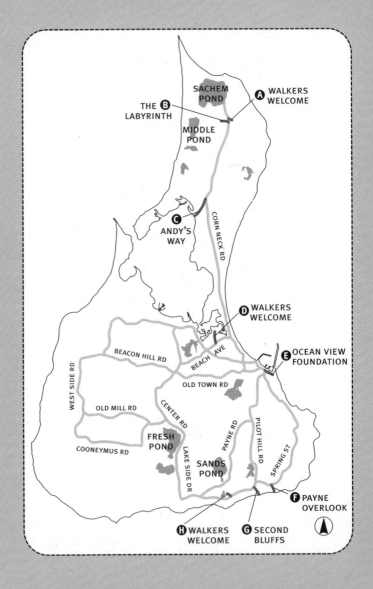

Ⓐ WALKERS WELCOME

SACHEM POND

ⒷTHE LABYRINTH

MIDDLE POND

CORN NECK RD

Ⓒ ANDY'S WAY

Ⓓ WALKERS WELCOME

BEACON HILL RD

BEACH AVE

Ⓔ OCEAN VIEW FOUNDATION

WEST SIDE RD

OLD TOWN RD

OLD MILL RD

CENTER RD

PAYNE RD

PILOT HILL RD

SPRING ST

COONEYMUS RD

FRESH POND

LAKE SIDE DR

SANDS POND

Ⓕ PAYNE OVERLOOK

Ⓗ WALKERS WELCOME

Ⓖ SECOND BLUFFS

Roadways

Trail

Coastal Features

0   0.25   0.50   0.75   1

SHORT HIKES

If you are not inclined for a long hike, or you simply want a brief interlude in a beautiful natural setting, then the following places are perfect for short visits.

ATTWOOD PROPERTY Ⓐ

Approximately four-tenths of a mile north of the Hodge Family Preserve on the east side of Corn Neck Road, there is a granite marker welcoming walkers to take a jaunt to the top of a hill where there are wonderful views of Sachem Pond, Cow Cove, Sandy Point and North Light. The Attwood Family donated this property to the Block Island Conservancy and it was opened to walkers in 2002.

THE LABYRINTH Ⓑ

A different, but equally spectacular view of the northern tip of the Island is located directly across the road from the Attwood Property. The owner of the property here, Barbara MacDougall, created a labyrinth to provide a place for spiritual exploration based on rituals going back to the ancient Greeks. You can compare the labyrinth here with the maze on the other side of Corn Neck Road. A labyrinth usually has one entrance, with no options for taking different paths and no mystery about the destination. The purpose is to find yourself. A maze is a walking puzzle with lots of choices about paths and directions. By contrast, the purpose is to lose yourself. Both labyrinths and mazes have strong symbolic connections to the culture of islands.

ANDY'S WAY Ⓒ

Andy's Way was donated by Al and the late Norma Starr in memory of their son who loved this special place, a favorite destination of those shellfishing for quahogs and soft-shelled clams. At low tide, it is one of the best spots on the Island to observe shore birds, among them the state-endangered American oystercatcher, which has an orange bill. It makes a continuous call while flying. In the northeastern part of the property is the largest un-ditched salt marsh in Rhode Island and a place where you can spot the state-endangered black-crowned night heron. To find Andy's Way, head north on Corn Neck Road a mile and a half north of the Beach Avenue intersection and look for the small hand-painted sign on the left. It is past the barn and fields of Mitchell Farm.

DUNN'S BRIDGE PATH D

Near the intersection of Corn Neck Road, on Beach Avenue is Dunn's Bridge. On the inland side of the bridge, just off the north side of the road, is a green sign welcoming walkers to explore this peninsula in Harbor Pond. The trail goes directly to the shore of the pond. The water here is brackish, meaning that its level changes with the tides and it is a combination of fresh and salt water. The Block Island Conservancy owns the property and manages it for the use and enjoyment of the public.

OCEAN VIEW FOUNDATION E

If you are in town and desire a pleasant walk to a quiet spot where you can enjoy the nature of Block Island that is both close to but completely removed from the bustle of the main street, simply find the trail located between the Post Office building and Ballard's Inn. After a short walk up the hill, you come upon a wooden pavilion with an elevated prospect of the village, Clay Head and the Atlantic Ocean. The trail loops through the foundation of the Ocean View Hotel, once the largest of the elegant hotels built on the Island during the Victorian Era. This former seaside resort burned to the ground in 1966, thereby removing from the landscape one of the Island's most prominent and historic structures. On this site, the Ocean View Foundation hosts daily programs in the summer including a popular weekly bird banding demonstration. Information about these events can be found on the bulletin board where the pavilion path leaves the street or in the *Block Island Times*.

EDWARD SANDS PAYNE OVERLOOK F

This property, once part of the Payne Farm, was purchased from members of the Payne Family by the State of Rhode Island with the assistance of The Nature Conservancy in the early 1980s. The parking lot is marked by a sign. When you follow the short path to the bluff's edge you will find yourself 200 feet above the surf of the Atlantic Ocean. To your left is the Southeast Light. There are stairs by the overlook to access the beach. The wind and waves continually pound these steps and they must be maintained to prevent further erosion of the fragile bluffs.

The Mohegan Bluffs are *bluffs* not *cliffs* because they are made of clay, sand, gravel, and soil or glacial till, not rock. The rapid erosion is primarily due to four factors: heavy rain and wind; powerful waves from the ocean below; groundwater seepage from above; and human traffic. Many birds, such as the bank swallow and barn owl, nest in the bluffs. This is one of three places on Block Island where the rare clay banks tiger beetle can be found. These three locations are the only places in Rhode Island where this species is recorded. This area is classified as a terminal moraine because it is near where the glacier stopped and began to recede, leaving the spectacular exposed bluffs to face the open ocean. The Atlantic Ocean extends from here to Portugal in the east. There is no land between Block Island and Europe.

SECOND BLUFFS (CHALET POINT) G

The other main public access point to the bluffs is owned by the Town of New Shoreham, the formal name for Block Island. It is located directly across from the intersection of Pilot Hill Road, an unpaved road, and Mohegan Trail. As at the Payne Overlook, a brief walk through coastal shrubs takes you to a vantage point high above the Atlantic. To your left (east) is the Southeast Light; to the right (southwest) is Montauk Point, in New York State. The name for this place, Chalet Point, alludes to a structure that blew down during Hurricane Carol in 1954, a reminder of how exposed and vulnerable this area is.

MURPHY/CORMIER H

On the inland side of Mohegan Trail, three-tenths of a mile west of Chalet Point, is another property owned and managed by the Block Island Conservancy for public enjoyment. Look for the "Walkers Welcome" sign marking the short trail leading to the top of a hill which offers dramatic views of the Island, the ocean, and Montauk Point, the easternmost tip of Long Island, in the distance.

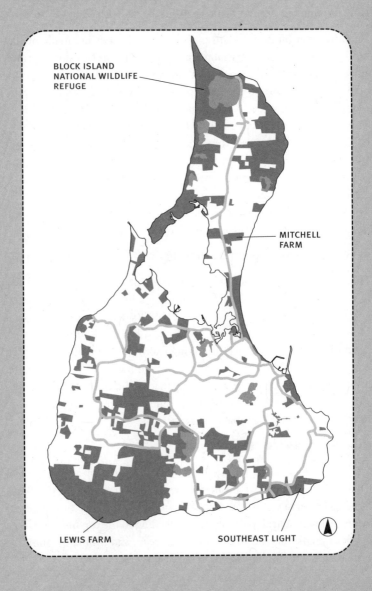

BLOCK ISLAND
NATIONAL WILDLIFE
REFUGE

MITCHELL
FARM

LEWIS FARM   SOUTHEAST LIGHT

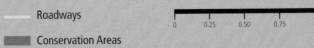

—— Roadways

⬛ Conservation Areas

⬛ Ponds

—— Coastal Features

0   0.25   0.50   0.75   1

OTHER CONSERVATION AREAS OF INTEREST

LEWIS FARM

Lewis Farm Preserve is home to the highest concentration of endangered species on Block Island and, for that matter, in the entire state of Rhode Island. The open-field habitat on the farm is particularly fragile and susceptible to overuse. As a result, the farm is a focal point for scientific research, primarily managed for endangered-species protection, and it is not open to the public for recreational uses. For information about occasional guided field walks on the farm, please contact The Nature Conservancy.

MITCHELL FARM

Mitchell Farm is one of the most visible conservation areas on Block Island. Located along Corn Neck Road, its gambrel-roofed barn, 200-year-old farmhouse, and open pastures with cows often grazing, preserve a historic New England rural landscape that is a favorite of painters and photographers. The fields run from the road all the way to Crescent Beach and provide a vital green belt through an area that has become one of the more intensely developed on the Island. The land is private and continues to be farmed by its owner, with a conservation easement over the fields held by the Block Island Conservancy.

SOUTHEAST LIGHT

The Southeast Light was built here in the early 1870s to warn mariners of the dangerous rocks and shoals. The brick lighthouse was rescued in 1993 and rolled intact 200 feet back from the eroding bluffs. The spot where the building once stood is marked by a large boulder, which is now only a few feet from the bluff. At one point this spot was 300 feet from the edge. The lighthouse was re-lit and returned to service as an aid-to-navigation in 1994. In 1997, it was designated a National Historic Landmark. The Southeast Light and grounds are open to the public for tours and will soon house a museum and bed and breakfast when interior renovations are completed.

WEST BEACH, THE BLOCK ISLAND NATIONAL WILDLIFE REFUGE & NORTH LIGHT

The perimeter of the western side of the "neck" of Block Island is comprised of a variety of lands in public and private ownership that form the Block Island National Wildlife Refuge. This is critical habitat for a number of migratory birds, rare plants, and nesting birds found on the beaches; it is also home to a state-endangered wading bird colony at Beane Point. Due to the sensitivity of the bird colony, Beane Point is closed to the public. Access to the refuge is at the end of West Beach Road and at Settlers Rock, where many people hike to the North Light and Sandy Point.

The dune field south of Sandy Point, a fine example of this habitat type, is a major rookery for the nearly two thousand great black-backed and herring gulls (with more than 600 gull nests). When the gulls are nesting (May through July) be sure to give them a wide berth because they will get aggressive if you get too close.

There is an interpretive center at the North Light that is open during the day in the summer. When on the beach, please stay away from the dunes and sensitive beach vegetation. Cow Cove is an excellent spot to observe shorebirds on migration in late summer and fall. Sachem Pond, the body of water west of Corn Neck Road at the tip of the Island, harbors a variety of migratory waterfowl from fall to spring.

Conservation Groups
Working on Block Island

The hallmark of the conservation effort on Block Island has been part-nerships; individual groups have been willing to work together toward a common purpose. It is important to note that the Town of New Shoreham, its government and citizens have been key partners in the conservation effort. Following is a description of the primary organizations that have been and continue to be active in conservation on the Island.

AUDUBON SOCIETY OF RHODE ISLAND
12 Sanderson Road
Smithfield, Rhode Island 02917
(401) 949-5454

The Audubon Society of Rhode Island (ASRI), founded in 1897, is the oldest environmental group in the state. ASRI is not associated with National Audubon and is an independent state-wide nonprofit organi-zation with headquarters in Smithfield, Rhode Island. Audubon's mis-sion is "to foster conservation of wild birds and other animals and plant life, to conserve wildlife habitat and unique natural areas... [and] to carry out a broad spectrum of public environmental education programs." On Block Island, the Audubon Society owns and manages conserved land. For many years, the society has sponsored a popular birding weekend during the fall migration in early October.

BLOCK ISLAND CONSERVANCY
P.O. Box 84
Block Island, Rhode Island 02807
(401) 466-3111

The Block Island Conservancy (BIC), founded in 1972, is a local grass-roots organization relying on its memberships and donations to support its conservation efforts. BIC's mission is "to maintain habitat for birds and animals, to protect the view of hills rolling to the sea, [and] to provide walking trails and quiet recreation to islanders and visitors." The Block Island Conservancy is a private nonprofit with a 12-person volunteer board of directors made up of its members.

BLOCK ISLAND LAND TRUST
P.O. Box 220
Block Island, Rhode Island 02807
(401) 466-3207

The Block Island Land Trust (BILT) is a municipal conservation organization that was created by state-enabling legislation in 1986. The trust is now funded by a three-percent transfer fee on all real estate transactions, and it has the ability, with town approval, to borrow money by issuing bonds for purposes of land conservation. The BILT has five trustees who are elected by town voters. The BILT's mission is "to protect ecologically sensitive areas, open space and land for agricultural use, preserve views sheds, and provide recreational opportunities."

THE NATURE CONSERVANCY
P.O. Box 1287
Block Island, Rhode Island 02807
(401) 466-2129

The Nature Conservancy (TNC) is an international nonprofit land conservation organization with headquarters in Arlington, Virginia, and a state office in Providence, Rhode Island. The conservancy was founded in 1951 and its mission is "to preserve plants, animals and natural communities that represent the diversity of life on Earth by protecting the lands and waters they need to survive." TNC has been working on Block Island since the 1970s. The organization works with local, state, federal government agencies and other nonprofits to protect and manage properties. The conservancy hired staff and opened an office on Block Island in 1991. The office is located on High Street, within walking distance of the village in Old Harbor. Be sure to check out the Visitors Center, which is open in the summer months.

OCEAN VIEW FOUNDATION
P. O. Box 291
Block Island, Rhode Island 02807
(401) 466-2224

The Ocean View Foundation was founded in 1999 to connect Island residents and visitors to nature through environmental education. The Foundation maintains a pavilion behind the Post Office building near the site of the former Ocean View Hotel. It sponsors a series of events throughout the year and is particularly known for excellent summer programs.

73

RHODE ISLAND DEPARTMENT OF ENVIRONMENTAL MANAGEMENT
Division of Parks and Recreation
2321 Hartford Ave
Johnston, Rhode Island 02919
(401) 222-2632

The Rhode Island Department of Environmental Management (DEM) is the agency charged with protecting and managing the state's environment and natural resources. The DEM administers federal and state funds for the protection of open space and agricultural lands. Funds from these sources have played a major role in the preservation effort on the Island. The DEM's goals on Block Island are "to provide recreational opportunities, to preserve areas for fish and wildlife management, and to protect natural and cultural resources of statewide importance."

74

UNITED STATES FISH & WILDLIFE SERVICE
50 Bend Road
Charlestown, Rhode Island 02813
(401) 364-9124

The United States Fish & Wildlife Service is a bureau of the federal government's Department of the Interior. The Fish & Wildlife Service is "the principal Federal agency responsible for conserving, protecting and enhancing fish, wildlife and plants and their habitats for the continuing benefit of the American people." The service enforces federal wildlife laws and is charged with the protection of endangered species. It also manages the 93 million-acre National Wildlife System, which includes the Block Island National Wildlife Refuge. The refuge includes properties between Sandy Point and the channel of Great Salt Pond. For information about all of the United States Fish & Wildlife refuges in Rhode Island, including Block Island, you might want to visit the new Kettle Pond Visitors Center in Charlestown, located off U.S. Route 1 midway between Westerly Airport and Point Judith, where the ferries depart for Block Island.

Animal & Plant Species Lists

The following are animals and plants that occur on Block Island.

KEY

C	Common	X	Extremely Rare	SP	Spring
FC	Fairly Common	?	Unknown	S	Summer
R	Rare			F	Fall
				W	Winter

CHECKLIST OF BLOCK ISLAND MAMMALS

Species	Status	Season
House Mouse	C	SP,S,F,W
White-footed Mouse	C	SP,S,F,W
Muskrat	FC	SP,S,F,W
Norway Rat	C	SP,S,F,W
Block Island Meadow Vole	FC	SP,S,F,W
White-tailed Deer	C	SP,S,F,W
Little Brown Bat	FC	SP,S,F
Silver-haired Bat	C	SP,S,F
Eastern Pipistrelle	?	SP,S,F
Harbor Seal	C	S,F,W
Gray Seal	R	W
Hooded Seal	X	W
Harp Seal	R	W

Silver-haired Bat

Birds at Beane Point

CHECKLIST OF BLOCK ISLAND BIRDS

Additional information
(N) Nesting   (M) May nest

Species	Status	Season
Red-throated Loon	FC	W
Common Loon	C	SP,F,W
Pied-billed Grebe	FC	SP,F,W
Horned Grebe	R	SP,F,W
Red-necked Grebe	R	SP,F,W
Northern Fulmar	X	SP,F,W
Cory's Shearwater	X	SP,S,F
Greater Shearwater	X	SP,S,F
Sooty Shearwater	X	SP,S,F
Manx Shearwater	X	SP,S,F
Wilson's Storm Petrel	X	SP,S,F
Northern Gannet	R	SP,F,W
Great Cormorant	FC	SP,F,W
Double-crested Cormorant	C	SP,S,F
American Bittern (N)	X	SP,S,F
Least Bittern	X	SP,S,F
Great Blue Heron (M)	C	SP,S,F,W
Great Egret (N)	FC	SP,S,F
Snowy Egret (N)	FC	SP,S,F
Little Blue Heron	R	SP,F
Cattle Egret	R	SP,F
Green-backed Heron (N)	R	SP,S,F

Black-crowned Nt. Heron (N)	C	SP,S,F
Yellow-crowned Nt. Heron (N)	FC	SP,S,F
Glossy Ibis	X	S
Mute Swan (N)	FC	SP,S,F,W
Snow Goose	FC	SP,F
Brant	FC	SP,F,W
Canada Goose (N)	C	SP,S,F,W
Wood Duck (N)	R	SP,S,F
Green-winged Teal	R	SP,F
American Black Duck (N)	C	SP,S,F,W
Mallard (N)	C	SP,S,F,W
Northern Pintail	R	SP,F
Blue-winged Teal	R	SP,F
Northern Shoveler	R	SP,F
Gadwall (N)	FC	SP,S,F,W
American Wigeon	R	SP,F,W
Redhead	R	SP,F
Ring-necked Duck	FC	SP,F
Greater Scaup	FC	SP,F,W
Lesser Scaup	FC	SP,F,W
Common Eider (M)	FC	SP,F,W
King Eider	X	W
Harlequin Duck	X	SP,F
Oldsquaw	R	SP,F
Black Scoter	R	SP,F,W
Surf Scoter	R	SP,F,W
White-winged Scoter	R	SP,F,W
Common Goldeneye	C	W
Bufflehead	C	SP,F,W
Hooded Merganser	X	W
Common Merganser	C	SP,F,W
Red-breasted Merganser	C	SP,F,W
Ruddy Duck	X	F,W
Turkey Vulture	X	SP,F
Osprey (N)	FC	SP,S,F
Bald Eagle	R	S
Northern Harrier (N)	C	SP,S,F,W
Sharp-shinned Hawk	C	SP,F
Cooper's Hawk (N)	FC	SP,F,W
Red-tailed Hawk	X	SP,F,W
American Kestrel	FC	SP,S,F

77

Merlin	FC	SP,F
Peregrine Falcon	FC	SP,F
Ring-necked Pheasant (N)	C	SP,S,F,W
Clapper Rail (M)	R	SP,S,F
Virginia Rail (N)	X	SP,S,F
Sora	R	SP,F
Common Moorhen	FC	SP,F
American Coot	FC	SP,F
Black-bellied Plover	C	SP,F
Lesser Golden Plover	R	SP,F
Semipalmated Plover	FC	SP,F
Piping Plover (M)	FC	SP,F
Killdeer (N)	FC	SP,S,F
American Oystercatcher (N)	C	SP,S,F
Greater Yellowlegs	FC	SP,S,F
Lesser Yellowlegs	R	SP,F
Solitary Sandpiper	X	SP,F
Willet (N)	FC	SP,S,F
Spotted Sandpiper	R	SP,F
Upland Sandpiper	X	SP,S,F
Whimbrel	R	SP,F
Ruddy Turnstone	FC	SP,F
Sanderling	C	SP,F,W
Semipalmated Sandpiper	FC	SP,F
Least Sandpiper	R	SP,F
White-rumped Sandpiper	X	SP,F
Baird's Sandpiper	X	SP,F
Pectoral Sandpiper	X	SP,F
Purple Sandpiper	X	SP,F
Dunlin	R	SP,F
Stilt Sandpiper	X	SP,F
Short-billed Dowitcher	R	SP,F
Long-billed Dowitcher	R	SP,F
Common Snipe (M)	R	SP,F
American Woodcock (N)	C	SP,S,F
Red Phalarope	X	SP,F
Pomarine Jaeger	X	SP,S,F
Parasitic Jaeger	X	SP,S,F
Laughing Gull	R	SP,F
Ring-billed Gull	R	SP,F
Herring Gull (N)	C	SP,S,F,W

78

Great Black-backed Gull (N)	C	SP,S,F,W
Black-legged Kittiwake	X	W
Caspian Tern	R	SP,F
Royal Tern	X	SP,F
Roseate Tern	R	SP,F
Common Tern	FC	SP,F
Least Tern	FC	SP,F
Forster's Tern	R	SP,F
Black Tern	X	SP,F
Black Skimmer	X	SP,F
Dovekie	X	W
Razorbill	X	W
Common Murre	X	W
Mourning Dove (N)	C	SP,S,F,W
Black-billed Cuckoo (M)	FC	SP,S,W
Yellow-billed Cuckoo (M)	R	SP,S,W
Barn Owl (N)	C	SP,S,F,W
Snowy Owl	X	W
Short-eared Owl	X	SP,F
Northern Saw-whet Owl	C	F,W
Common Nighthawk	R	SP,F
Chimney Swift	FC	SP,F
Ruby-th. Hummingbird (M)	R	SP,F,W
Belted Kingfisher (N)	C	SP,S,F
Red-headed Woodpecker	X	SP,S,F
Red-bellied Woodpecker	R	SP,F
Yellow-bellied Sapsucker	FC	SP,F
Downy Woodpecker (N)	FC	SP,S,F,W
Hairy Woodpecker	R	SP,F
Common Flicker (N)	C	SP,S,F,W
Eastern Wood-pewee	FC	SP,F
Yellow-bellied Flycatcher	FC	SP,F
Acadian Flycatcher	R	SP,F
Traill's Flycatcher	FC	SP,F
Least Flycatcher	FC	SP,F
Eastern Phoebe	C	SP,F
Great Crested Flycatcher	R	SP,F
Eastern Kingbird (N)	FC	SP,S,F
Horned Lark	R	SP,F,W
Purple Martin	R	SP,F
Tree Swallow (N)	FC	SP,S,F

Rough-winged Swallow (N)	FC	SP,S,F
Bank Swallow (N)	C	SP,S,F
Barn Swallow (N)	FC	SP,S,F
Blue Jay (N)	C	SP,S,F,W
American Crow (N)	C	SP,S,F,W
Fish Crow (N)	R	SP,S,F
Black-capped Chickadee (N)	C	SP,S,F,W
Red-breasted Nuthatch (M)	C	SP,S,F,W
White-breasted Nuthatch	FC	SP,F,W
Brown Creeper	C	SP,F
Carolina Wren (N)	C	SP,S,F,W
House Wren (N)	FC	SP,S,F
Winter Wren	FC	SP,F,W
Marsh Wren (N)	R	SP,S,F
Golden-crowned Kinglet	C	SP,F,W
Ruby-crowned Kinglet	FC	SP,F,W
Blue-gray Gnatcatcher	R	SP,F
Eastern Bluebird	FC	SP,F
Veery	FC	SP,F
Gray-cheeked Thrush	R	SP,F
Swainson's Thrush	FC	SP,F
Hermit Thrush	FC	SP,F,W
Wood Thrush (M)	R	SP,F
American Robin (N)	C	SP,S,F,W
Gray Catbird (N)	C	SP,S,F
Northern Mockingbird (N)	C	SP,S,F,W
Brown Thrasher (N)	FC	SP,S,F,W
Cedar Waxwing (N)	C	SP,S,F,W
Northern Shrike	R	W

80

Prairie Warbler

European Starling (N)	C	SP,S,F,W
White-eyed Vireo (N)	FC	SP,S,F
Blue-headed Vireo	FC	SP,F
Yellow-throated Vireo	R	SP,F
Warbling Vireo	FC	SP,F
Philadelphia Vireo	FC	SP,F
Red-eyed Vireo	C	SP,F
Blue-winged Warbler	R	SP,F
Golden-winged Warbler	R	SP,F
Tennessee Warbler	FC	SP,F
Orange-crowned Warbler	R	SP,F
Nashville Warbler	FC	SP,F
Northern Parula	FC	SP,F
Yellow Warbler (N)	FC	SP,S,F
Chestnut-sided Warbler	FC	SP,F
Magnolia Warbler	C	SP,F
Cape May Warbler	R	SP,F
Black-throated Blue Warbler	C	SP,F
Yellow-rumped Warbler	C	SP,F,W
Black-throated Green Warbler	FC	SP,F
Blackburian Warbler	R	SP,F
Pine Warbler	FC	SP,F,W
Prairie Warbler	FC	SP,F
Palm Warbler	R	SP,F
Bay-breasted Warbler	FC	SP,F
Blackpoll Warbler	C	SP,F
Cerulean Warbler	X	SP,F
Black-and-White Warbler	C	SP,F
American Redstart (M)	C	SP,F
Worm-eating Warbler	R	SP,F
Ovenbird	C	SP,F
Northern Waterthrush	C	SP,F
Kentucky Warbler	R	SP,F
Connecticut Warbler	R	SP,F
Mourning Warbler	R	SP,F
Common Yellowthroat (N)	C	SP,S,F
Hooded Warbler	R	SP,F
Wilson's Warbler	FC	SP,F
Canada Warbler	FC	SP,F
Yellow-breasted Chat	R	SP,F
Summer Tanager	X	SP,F

81

Scarlet Tanager .... FC .... SP,F
Northern Cardinal (N) .... C .... SP,S,F,W
Rose-breasted Grosbeak .... FC .... SP,F
Blue Grosbeak .... X .... SP,F
Indigo Bunting .... FC .... SP,F
Dickcissel .... R .... SP,F,W
Eastern Towhee (N) .... C .... SP,S,F
Chipping Sparrow (N) .... FC .... SP,F
Clay-colored Sparrow .... R .... SP,F
Lark Sparrow .... R .... SP,F
Savannah Sparrow (N) .... FC .... SP,S,F,W
Grasshopper Sparrow (N) .... R .... SP,S,F
Salt-marsh Sharp-tailed Sparrow (N) .... FC .... SP,S,F,W
Fox Sparrow .... R .... W
Song Sparrow (N) .... C .... SP,S,F,W
Lincoln's Sparrow .... FC .... SP,F
Swamp Sparrow .... FC .... SP,F
White-throated Sparrow .... C .... SP,F,W
White-crowned Sparrow .... R .... SP,F
Slate-colored Junco .... C .... SP,F,W
Lapland Longspur .... R .... SP,F
Snow Bunting .... FC .... SP,F,W
Bobolink .... R .... SP,F,W
Red-winged Blackbird (N) .... C .... SP,S,F
Eastern Meadowlark .... FC .... SP,F,W
Yellow-headed Blackbird .... X .... S
Rusty Blackbird .... R .... SP,F
Common Grackle (N) .... C .... SP,S,F,W
Brown-headed Cowbird (N) .... C .... SP,S,F,W
Baltimore Oriole (M) .... FC .... SP,F
Orchard Oriole (M) .... R .... SP,S,F
Purple Finch .... FC .... SP,F
House Finch (N) .... C .... SP,S,F,W
White-winged Crossbill .... R .... W
Common Redpoll .... R .... W
Pine Siskin .... R .... SP,F,W
American Goldfinch (N) .... C .... SP,F
House Sparrow (N) .... C .... SP,S,F,W

82

CHECKLIST OF BLOCK ISLAND REPTILES

Species	Status	Season
Northern Water Snake	FC	SP,S,F
Brown Snake	FC	SP,S,F
Eastern Garter Snake	C	SP,S,F
Eastern Painted Turtle	C	SP,S,F
Snapping Turtle	C	SP,S,F
Spotted Turtle	R	SP,S,F
Eastern Box Turtle	X	SP,S,F

83

CHECKLIST OF BLOCK ISLAND AMPHIBIANS

Species	Status	Season
Red-spotted Newt	R	SP,S,F
Green Frog	FC	SP,S,F
Spring Peeper	C	SP,S,F

CHECKLIST OF BLOCK ISLAND INSECTS

This is a list of the insects most likely to be seen while hiking. It is by no means complete. (In fact, we are still finding species that have never been recorded on Block Island!)

Species	Status	Season
BUTTERFLIES		
Tiger Swallowtail	C	S
Monarch	C	SP,S,F
Viceroy	FC	SP,S,F
Pearl Crescent	FC	S
American Copper	C	S
Spring Azure	C	SP
Diana	FC	S
Cabbage White	C	S
Clouded Sulphur	C	SP,S,F
Red Admiral	FC	S
MOTHS		
Io	C	SP,S
Polyphemus	C	SP,S
Luna	FC	S
One-eyed Sphinx	FC	SP,S
Hummingbird Clearwing	C	S
Virgin Tiger	FC	SP,S

DAMSELFLIES

| Eastern Forktail | C | SP,S |
| Familiar Bluet | C | SP,S |

DRAGONFLIES

Calico Pennant	C	SP,S
Eastern Amberwing	C	SP,S
Eastern Pondhawk	C	SP,S
Seaside Dragonlet	FC	SP,S
Ruby Meadowhawk	C	S,F
Carolina Saddlebags	FC	SP,S
Common Green Darner	C	S,F

BEETLES

Japanese Beetle	C	S
Lady Beetle	C	SP,S,F
Rhinoceros Beetle	C	S,F

84

Ruby Meadowhawk

CHECKLIST OF BLOCK ISLAND SPIDERS

This is a list of the spiders most likely to be seen while hiking. It is by no means complete. (In fact, we are still finding species that have never been recorded on Block Island!)

Species	Status	Season
Shamrock	C	S,F
Black and Yellow Argiope	FC	S,F
Grass	C	SP,S,F
Daring Jumping	C	SP,S,F
Six-spotted Fishing	FC	SP,S,F
Carolina Wolf	FC	SP,S,F

CHECKLIST OF BLOCK ISLAND PLANTS

This is a list of the plants most likely to be seen while hiking. (It is also by no means complete.)

Species	Status
BEACH	
Sea Lavender	FC
Beach Rose	C
Seaside Goldenrod	C
Sea Rocket	FC
Dusty Miller	C
Beach Pea	C
Beach Plum	FC
MEADOW	
Blackberry	C
Dewberry	C
Strawberry	FC
Black-eyed Susan	C
New York Aster	C
New England Aster	C
Common Aster	C
Common Milkweed	FC
Panic Grass	FC
Butterfly Weed	R
Butter-and-Eggs	C
Rough-leaved Goldenrod	C
Lance-leaved Goldenrod	C
Yarrow	C
Queen Anne's Lace	C
Pasture Rose	FC
Bull Thistle	FC
MORAINAL GRASSLAND	
Bushy Rockrose	R
Northern Blazing Star	FC
Little Bluestem	C
SHRUBLAND	
Shadbush	C
Bayberry	C
Northern Arrowwood	C
Pokeweed	C
Winterberry	C

Multiflora Rose.. C
Black Chokeberry C
Sweet Greenbrier .... FC

WETLAND

Fragrant Water-lily..................................... C
Swamp Azalea.. FC
Sweet Pepperbush.. FC
Swamp Milkweed... FC
Buttonbush C
Phragmities... C
Water Willow... C

TREES

Beech.. R
Black Gum.. R
Black Cherry C
Horse Chestnut .... FC
Chinese Chestnut.. FC
Sycamore Maple.. C
Japanese Black Pine C
Hawthorn... FC
Apple .... FC
Eastern Red Cedar C

VINES

Asian Bittersweet.. C
Poison Ivy.. C
Virginia Creeper.. FC
Black Swallowwort...................................... FC
Japanese Honeysuckle................................ FC

Poison Ivy grows along many Block Island trails. If it has "leaves of three, let it be."

Field notes

Field notes

Field notes

INDEX

Page numbers in bold indicate photo.

Adrian House 24
Alder, black 27
American Bird Conservancy 6
Anderson, Eva xi, 95
Andy's Way 65-67
Apple tree 13, 47
Arrowwood 37, **38**
Asch Family xii, 30
Aster, common 41, **42**
Atlantic Ocean 3, 20, 34, 44, 67, 68
Attwood:
    Family xii, 66
    Property 65, 66
Audubon Society of Rhode Island
    viii, 72
Ball:
    Farm 3
    Lewis Property 45
    Lucretia Mott viii, 22, 24
    Martha xi
Ball-O'Brien Park 18, 20
Bat, silver-haired 75
Bayberry 27, 37
Beach Avenue 67
Beacon Hill:
    Homeowners Association xi, 18
    Road 18, 19, 22, 23
    View of 5, 6
Beane Point 71, **76**
Beech 31
Beetle:
    American burying 5, 19, **35**
    Turpentine 24
Blackberry **93**
Black Rock:
    Preserve 16, 29-34, 37
    Road 30, 31, 34
    Rock 35
    Trail 29-34, 36
Blackbird, red-winged 37
Blazing star, northern 27, 28

Block Island:
    Conservancy viii, xi, 8, 12, 18, 22, 34, 44, 45, 66, 67, 68, 70, 72, 95
    Historical Society 24
    Land Trust viii, 8, 20, 26, 31, 40, 73, 95
    Power Company 37
    School 24, 40, 41, 95
    State Airport 22, 23
Bluebird, eastern 10
Breakers 13
Breed Land 9
Briar, sweet green 24
Bullhead, brown 3
Catbird, gray 19, 24, 41
Cattail marsh 12, 13
Center Road 20
Chalet Point (Second Bluffs) 65, 68
Champlin:
    Farm **59**
    Foundations 40, 95
    Road 18
Cherry, black 27
Chestnut, Chinese 24
Chickadee, black-capped 3, 27
Church, Isaac 37
Clay Head:
    Long Lot Trail 5, 6, 10
    Preserve vi, 1-6, 8, 13, 20, 41, **50**, 67
    Swamp 3, **57**
    Trail 2, 3, 5
Comings, Scott B. 95
Connecticut Avenue 12
Cooneymus Road 30, 31, 34, 36, 37, 40, 44, 45
Cooneymus Road Link 29-34
Cormier Family xii
Corn Neck Road 2-5, 8, 10, 66, 67, 70, 71
Cow Cove 10, 66, 71
Crescent Beach 6, 20, **62**, 70
Crow:
    American 23
    Fish 23
Darner, common green 27, 41
Deer, white-tailed 19, 28, 41

90

Dickens Farm:
    Preserve 43-47, **52**
    Road 44, 45
    Trail 43-**47**
Dickens, Elizabeth vii, 44, 45
Dodge:
    Cemetery 26-28
    Earl 22
    George 10
    Winfield 44
Drumlin 13
Duck:
    American black 27
    Wood 23
Dunn's Bridge Path 65, 67
DuPont, Anne F. H. 22
Eagle, bald 37
Edward S. Payne Overlook 65, 67, 68
Elaine Loffredo Preserve **x**, 25-28
Enchanted Forest 22, 23
Erlanger Family xi, 18
Flicker, yellow-shafted 3
Fresh Pond 30, 34-37, 40
Fresh Pond Trail 31, 40
Fresh Swamp Trail 36, 39-42
Frog, green 27, 34, 37
Forktail, lilypad 23
Gasner's Pond **61**
Gayfeather 27
Georgian Swamp **58**
Ginkgo 31
Glacial outwash channel 34
Great Salt Pond vii, 6, 13, 16, 18,
    20, 30
Great Salt Pond to Beacon Hill Road
    Link   17-20
Greenway Trail System vi, 15, 16, 18,
    22, 30, 36, 40, 95
Guerry Family xii, 30
Gull:
    Great black-backed 71
    Herring 71
Gum, black 31
Hall, Gene xii
Harbor Baptist Church 24
Harbor Pond 67

Harrier, northern 35, **46**, 37, 45
Harrison:
    Family xi, 18
    Loop 18
Hawk, Cooper's 5
Hawkweed, mouse-ear 27
Hawthorn 24
Heron:
    Great blue 4, 27
    Green 27
Herring, Charlotte xi
High Street 40, 73
Highview Inn 13
Hodge Family Wildlife Preserve
    xv, 2-4, 7-10, 66
Hull Pond **60**
Hunting xvii
Hygeia House 13
Indian Cemetery 37, 40
Isaac's Corner 37
Island Cemetery 18, 20
Ivy, poison **xvii, 86**
Jones:
    Family xii
    Property 31, **32**
    Walter 31
Jules and Doris Stein Foundation
    xii, 22
Kelly, Cindy 24
King, Burt and Melanie xii, 26
Labyrinth 65, 66
Lakeside Drive 36, 37, 40
Lang, Keith H. 95
Lapham:
    Elise xii, 2, 5, 6
    Family ix, xi, 3, 4, 6, 50
    F. David xii, 2, 5, 6
Larkin, Dan and Jean xii, 27
Lewis:
    Alyce xi, 12
    Captain John R. **iii**, viii, xi, 12
    Clarence 45, 47
    David xii
    Farm 28, 31, 37, 45, 47, **52**, 69, 70
    Keith viii, xii
    William xii, 45

Little Sachem 4, 5
Littlefield:
   Christopher vi, xi, xii
   Farm 3, **49**, **57**
Locust, black 31
Loffredo:
   Elaine Preserve x, 25-28
   Robert xii
Lyme disease xvi
MacDougall, Barbara 66
Manisseans vii, 37
Mansion Beach 5
Maple, sycamore 3, 24
Marsh Hawk Hollow 22
Maze, The 2, 3, 5
McCluskey, Donald and Dorothy xii
Meadow Hill Greenway 11-14
Meadowhawk, ruby **84**
Meadowlark, eastern 41
Merlin **9**
Meiss, Margaret xii, 45
Middle Pond 9, 10
Milkweed, common 5, 9, 12, 41
Mitchell:
   Adrian vi, xi
   Farm vi, 67, 69, 70
Mohegan:
   Bluffs 3, 68
   Trail 68
Monarch:
   Butterfly 5, 27, 41
   Caterpillar 41
Montauk Point, Long Island 28, 68
Morainal grassland 23, 28, 34
Mott, Nathan 22
Murphy, Family xii
Murphy/Cormier short hike 65, 68
Nathan Mott Park viii, 18, 19, 21-24,
   26, 28, 30
Nathan Mott Park Corporation 22
National Wildlife Refuge 6, 10, 69,
   71, 74
Nature Conservancy, The vi, viii, xi,
   xii, xvi, xvii, 4, 5, 8, 22, 24, 26, 31,
   40, 67, 70, 73, 95
Needlegrass, purple 28

New Harbor 19, 20
New Shoreham, Town of viii, xii, 8,
   20, 68
Newt, red-spotted 23
Night Heron:
   Black-crowned 67
   Yellow-crowned 4
Norcross Foundation 40
North Beacon Trail 23
North Light 5, 6, 8, 10, **63**, 66, 69, 71
Oak, pin 31
Ocean View Foundation xii, 65, 67, 73
Old Harbor 3, 12, 23, 40, **62**, 73

92

Pokeweed

93

Old Mill:
   Road 22, 23, 26-28, 30
Link 29-34
Old Town Road 12
Oppenheimer:
   Hal xii, 22
   Sally Hamilton 22
Osprey 37
Owl, barn 6, 27, 68
Oystercatcher, American 67
Panero Family xii
Payne:
   Family 40, 67

Blackberry

Payne (continued):
   Farm 40, 41, 67
   Farm Trail 36, 39-42
Overlook 65, 67, 68
   Road 40
Peckham:
   Farm Homeowners Association
   xii, 36
   Pond 34
   Farm trail 31, 36
Peeper, spring 23
Penn:
   Arthur 37
   Deborah xii
Pets xvi
Pheasant, ring-necked 19, 27, 33
Phelan:
   Blake and Michele xii, 40
   William and Harriet xii, 40
Pike, F. Norris and Nancy xii
Pilot Hill Road 68
Pine, Japanese black 5, 24
Pokeweed 92
Pots and Kettles 4
Rail, Virginia 45
Reed and Barrell Families xii
Rhode Island Department of
   Environmental Management
   viii, 74
Risom:
   Family xi
   Jens xi
Rockrose, bushy 27
Rodman's Hollow vii, 3, 23, 26, 27,
   29-34, 36, 37, 48, 55
Rosenzweig, Laura xii
Sachem Pond 2, 6, 10, 54, 66
Sandy Point 66, 71
Sapsucker, yellow-bellied 13
Second Bluffs (Chalet Point) 65, 68
Settlers Rock 2, 71
Shadbush 12-14, 27, 34, 37
Shiner, golden 3
Shirley's Pond 26-28
Smilin' Thru 22, 36, 37, 40
Smith, Robert Ellis xi, xii

Snake, northern water 23
Soorikian Property 44, 45
South Beacon Hill Trail 18, 21-24
Southeast Light 5, 12, 24, 67-71
Sparrow:
   Savannah 33
   Song **19**, 41
   White-throated 20
Starr, Al and Norma xii, 66
Swallow, bank 4, 68
Swallowwort, black 24
Symbio Design xi, 95
Terminal moraine 68
Tiger beetle, clay banks 68
Tonner, Kurt and Erica xi, 18
Towhee, eastern 20, 24, 41
Turnip Farm Preserve 19, 22, 23,
   25-28, 30, 31, 34
Turtle, eastern painted 23, 37
U.S. Fish & Wildlife Service viii, 5,
   10, 74
Vole, Block Island meadow 23
Wagner:
   Michael xii
   Suzanne xii
Walling, Christopher xii, 18
Warbler:
   Golden-winged 20
   Prairie **80**
Yellow 3, 19
Weather Bureau 13
Weed, butterfly 41
West Beach 10, 69, 71
West Side Baptist Church, former
   26, 28
West Side Road 18, 20, 26-28, 30, 44
Win Dodge Trail 43-47
Winterberry 27
Wood, Peter & Shirley xii, 26, 30
Woodcock, American 8, 45
Wren, Carolina 3, **4**, 19, 41
Worden Pond 44
Yellowthroat, common 19, 20

Authors

KEITH H. LANG has been a trustee of the Block Island Land Trust and a director of the Block Island Conservancy. Keith was the first state director for The Nature Conservancy in Rhode Island; the Rhode Island Field Office, the Block Island Program, and the Greenway trail system were initiated during his tenure. He worked for many years for the late United States Senator John H. Chafee, most recently as director of his Rhode Island office. Keith is now executive director of The Champlin Foundations, Rhode Island-based charitable foundations whose areas of focus include funding land conservation.

SCOTT COMINGS graduated from Earlham College with a B.A. in biology and education. He is an accomplished ornithologist and has participated in a number of field studies, some of the accounts of which he has published. He is also the author of *The Nature of Block Island*, which was published in the summer of 2005. In addition to his position as director of The Nature Conservancy's Block Island Program, Scott is a field sciences teacher at the Block Island School, where he was recognized as Educator of the Year in 1999.

PRODUCTION TEAM

MAPS: Scott B. Comings and Symbio Design
PHOTOGRAPHS: All photographs by Keith H. Lang, except those by Scott B. Comings *(pp. xvii, 4, 9, 13, 19, 38, 42, 46, 75, 76, 80, 84, 86, 92, 93, back cover)*, Peter A. Schaefer *(p. 54)*, Andrea Kozol *(p. 33, back cover)* and Malcolm Greenaway *(p. iii)*
BOOK DESIGN: Symbio Design | Eva Anderson, art director

ENVIRONMENTAL NOTES: This book was printed with vegetable-based inks.

The text pages are printed on New Leaf Opaque 100, which is made with 100% post-consumer waste, processed chlorine free, and manufactured at a mill that uses bio-gas captured from the local landfill.

The color photo pages are printed on New Leaf Primavera Gloss, a paper made with 80% recycled content of which 40% is post-consumer waste, processed chlorine free.